THE OFFICIAL
COMPANION
SEASONS 3 & 4

**24: The Official Companion
Seasons 3& 4**

ISBN 1 84576 463 3
ISBN-13 9781845764630

Published by Titan Books,
a division of Titan Publishing Group Ltd
144 Southwark Street
London
SE1 0UP

First edition February 2007
10 9 8 7 6 5 4 3 2 1

24: The Official Companion Seasons 3 and 4
™ & © 2007 Twentieth Century Fox Film Corporation.
All rights reserved.
24 Produced in Association with REAL TIME PRODUCTIONS. IMAGINE
TELEVISION

Acknowledgements
James Badge Dale interview and portions of the Carlos Bernard interview provided by journalist
Bryan Cairns. Thanks!

The author would again like to extend her many thanks to the incredible team at Fox: Day Vinson,
Virginia King and Jenny Kay. Also, my sincere appreciation to Joel Surnow, Bob Cochran, Howard
Gordon and the entire crew of *24* for their generous access.
My personal thanks again goes out to all my friends and family, who continue to lead me through my
darkest days with love and humor, including: Alex, Hope, Len, and Angie & Tony. Also to the best
24 fans around: George, Jax and TwoGuysTalking – Mike and Brian. And to Gordon for always mak-
ing me laugh, sharing your talents and for your unfailing support and kindness. You are my heart.
Thank you.

The publishers would like to thank the cast (both past and present) and crew of *24* for all their help
with this book. A big thank you also to Virginia King and Rimma Aranovich at Twentieth Century Fox.

What did you think of this book? We love to hear from our readers. Please email us at:
readerfeedback@titanemail.com or write to us at the above address.
You can also visit us at **www.titanbooks.com**

To subscribe to our regular newsletter for up-to-the-minute news, great offers and competitions,
email: **booksezine@titanemail.com**

A CIP catalogue record for this title is available from the British Library.

Printed and bound in the USA.

The Official Companion
Seasons 3 & 4
Tara DiLullo

TITAN BOOKS

Contents

RETURN TO CTU

Creating Seasons 3 & 4

In about the time it takes a person to travel from New York City to Australia, Jack Bauer saved the life of a Presidential candidate, lost his wife to a murderous mole, prevented a nuclear bomb from detonating in Los Angeles, and helped stave off a retaliatory war. All in all, a rather exhausting forty-eight hours for a character that was quickly becoming an action icon for audiences around the world.

24 was becoming a hit, a serialized televisual page-turner that was defying critical predictions by gaining ratings ground every season. Who could have imagined that a show centering on a tragic yet intensely patriotic character named Jack Bauer would evolve into a media force to be reckoned with? Certainly not *24* co-creators and executive producers Joel Surnow and Robert Cochran, who still vividly remember their struggles to create an initial season storyline that would stretch for twenty-four episodes. Yet creative growing pains aside, their groundbreaking real time concept proved to be the second star of *24*, with the ever-ticking clock serving to inspire a fresh storytelling style and a furious momentum that swept audiences off their feet.

As the third season loomed, Surnow, Cochran and executive producer Howard Gordon prepared to tackle the question that faced them every May — where does Jack Bauer go next? "We wanted a different story after the radical Islam story in season two," Surnow explains. "A lot of stuff comes out of necessity on this show. We were short on Middle Eastern actors so we thought, 'Okay, there are a lot of Hispanic actors here in Los Angeles, so let's set up a South America drug story.' As soon as we started thinking about a drug story, we thought up the idea of Jack going undercover and becoming a drug addict. So that's the first burst of that season."

Robert Cochran says, "We were looking for a different

way into terrorism. Ultimately, with CTU, the 'T' stands for terrorism, so you've got to get there," he chuckles. "We had done some pretty straightforward stuff the first years, and we had all done some reading on narco-terrorism and the connection between the terrorists and the drug dealers, so we tried that angle. A lot of the narco-terrorism connections are over in Asia, but we can hardly do that. There are some in South America too but we can't send Jack to Brazil because he'd be on a plane for eight hours. So Mexico was the place we could reasonably get him back without too much time on a plane.

"Another thing that we always have to figure out is where to put Jack emotionally." Cochran continues, "Obviously, he's got his agent stuff to do but we want him to have a place emotionally to start from to give him a place to go. In this case, we were able to meld his agent stuff with the personal thing, which was him being a heroin addict. Theoretically, he addicted himself to heroin in order to be able to go undercover with this cartel, which had terrorist connections. It is in fact, in a plot sense, what happens. But at some point he's called out by Salazar who asks, 'Is that really why you did it? Or is there something in you that wanted to become addicted?' I think that's a theme there in Jack's life, which we've touched on a couple of other times. Once was in season

two, when he is flying the bomb into the desert and [George] Mason talks to him about the same thing: 'Do you want to die? Is life so difficult for you that it would be easier to end it all?' So that's a thing that's always fun for us to play with because the stuff Jack does build up such a burden, in terms of guilt and the losses he sustains, but the question he is always asking himself is, 'Is it worth going on?'"

Bauer's continuing friction with his daughter Kim also became a piece of the overarching theme for the year. Howard Gordon explains, "The season also came out of the fact that Jack would get emotionally in a place where he is enlisted back into the field and he embraces his work, but at the expense of having any kind of relationship. We brought back Kim and put her in CTU. Then we gave Jack an apprentice [Chase Edmunds] who was having a relationship with Kim and they illustrated the defiant idea that you can do this work and have human relationships." The *Romeo and Juliet* aspect of Kim's relationship also served to pull her character into the action, a yearly challenge for the writers. They even admit one of their glaring weaknesses has been how to use Kim in a way that doesn't alienate audiences. Cochran says, "In Jack's mind, [the relationship] wasn't good for her, so that worked well. Looking back on it, eventually we ended up putting her

in jeopardy again, because the truth of the matter is, that's where the real juice lies between a parent and a child. Ultimately, the real power is when she is in jeopardy, particularly if it's jeopardy that in some sense he feels he is responsible for. So we ended up going back to that same place, which I think worked fine."

Another major plot point for the year was explaining what happened to President David Palmer. The season two cliffhanger left him prone on the ground after being exposed to a flesh-eating virus and no one was certain if he survived... not even the writers. Gordon reveals, "We didn't know if we had a story for Palmer. We would not do that cliffhanger now, because we real-ly didn't know if he was dead or alive." The producers eventually came up with the implosion of his Presidency as a strong use for the character. Surnow says, "We kept him alive but he now has some shaky health issues. We then brought in his brother, Wayne Palmer." Gordon continues, "He was the RFK [Robert Kennedy] brother, who was his watch guard. From Palmer's shakiness, we then gave him a doctor and made her a woman and then a white woman, so there is no love lost between Wayne and Dr Anne Packard."

Surnow inserts with a smile, "We like to triangulate relationships: Jack, his daughter, her boyfriend and Palmer, his brother, his girlfriend."

With the major stories in place, the writer's room moved forward, but Gordon admits it was tough going. "We really struggled with the season until somewhere around episode twelve." A big stumbling block ended up being the big reveal that Jack, Tony Almeida and Hector Salazar were secretly working together. Surnow sighs, "We killed ourselves to make that work." Gordon laughs and concurs, "It was revealed in episode seven when Jack delivers Hector's brother and then they embrace. It was this big reveal that we killed ourselves over and it happened and people were like, 'So what?' The show is so squarely from Jack's point of view that in order to keep a secret from the audience for those episodes it felt like a cheat because you don't really know where Jack is."

By mid-season Surnow says the story then shifted from narcotics to the virus outbreak and, they all agree, that's when the season hit its stride. Gordon offers, "I think it got better when we got into the hotel. Another theme was with Michelle [Dessler] and Tony, who were

also having a relationship and they are tested." Cochran continues, "It was something we hadn't quite done before. It was the first time we had two agents in love, who had to make these tough decisions about each other. We liked that they made different decisions [in seasons three and four] when faced with the same question. In that situation, there is no right decision."

Evaluating the overall season, the writers are frank in offering what fell short. Cochran says, "I felt like the first part of season three wasn't great, but I think the last third of the season was really good. My own feeling was that it didn't work as well as we hoped because once we began to explore the narco aspect of the terrorism there was a lot of stuff that felt familiar. Not that that has to be bad, but a lot of our show lives in places where you don't see much like it on TV. We've seen a fair amount of the South American drug dealer thing on television and the movies. It was fine, the acting was terrific, but overall it didn't feel as unique as a lot of the other storylines we have been able to tell."

Surnow adds, "Having the audience out of Kiefer's point of view for five episodes hurt us. I think once we set off the terrorist on US soil, that's when it worked the best."

For his part, Gordon laments, "One of the missed opportunities of that season was Claudia [Salazar]. We had a whole story involving her where again we questioned whether Jack can have a relationship." Agreeing, Surnow adds, "It was the best onscreen kiss Kiefer had and they really played it. But she went off and did a movie so half these storylines are not dictated inside the writer's room."

The end of season three found Bauer and Palmer at their most vulnerable. After a season of deception, President Palmer decides not to run again. The complexity of that decision was a season highlight for Gordon. "I think there is a great moment when Sherry [Palmer] turns to him and she says, 'You called me,' and it illustrates their relationship. David was upstanding and all that, but when he needed it, he tasked someone to do what was necessary. There is an argument and she calls him on it and there is a moment on his face where he knows she is telling the truth. I always thought that was the end of his Presidency. It was the end of his innocence. He couldn't do the job either because of what it required and that's why he has a one term Presidency." "So he wasn't evil," Surnow clarifies. "He

just made a mistake."

In Jack's world, Kim and Chase decide to retire from CTU, and Gordon explains, "At the end, they reveal they are leaving together, so Jack is kind of right — you can't do the work and have a life." Overwhelmed by the day, the season ends with Bauer breaking down in his truck — a surprising moment of release for the character. Surnow explains, "We wanted a closure end of the season, as opposed to a cliffhanger. We thought instead of trying to do something big, we would try something small." With a smirk, he cracks, "Every other season, Jack has to end the season crying. He ended the first season crying and ended the third crying. He's a whiney baby."

The start of season four provided the creative team with some new challenges. Due to the intensely serialized structure of *24*, the Fox Network decided to move the series premiere to January 2005 and run the entire season uninterrupted until May. Now the season premiere became even more important in terms of hooking potential new viewers, and the writer's adjusted accordingly. Surnow explains, "We like to put our money behind the first four episodes. Now that we start in January over two nights, we spend more time rewriting the first two episodes than any other because we have so much hinging on the first two nights. In terms of audience, whomever we start with, we don't want to lose them by the end of the second night."

Creatively, the team moved the story along eighteen months and pulled out a big twist — Jack Bauer is happy. Cochran sets the stage. "Our thinking to start with was that since his daughter wasn't going to be around, he doesn't really have a strong emotional connection to anyone. If she's gone, he's going to be too much of a free agent. You want your hero to be emotionally connected to something. He's got to have something he cares about besides the job. We thought, 'Well what if he's fallen in love with this woman?' What he went through [in season three] was so traumatic for him professionally, the heroin addiction, that he's actually trying to change his life. Now he's got a desk job and a relationship with a woman [Audrey Raines], who really is a lovely person and you want him to succeed with it. It's a brand new place for Jack to be — he actually has a life for the first time almost since the first episode of season one. Of course, everyone knows it's

not going to last but at least it starts him out there."

With Jack's emotional state in place, the writers again toiled over developing the yearly threat. Gordon says, "Everyone was so happy with the end of season three because of the viruses. Now there always has to be a big threat and everyone was concerned — and I was one of them — that there was no big threat in season four. They kidnapped the Secretary of State, who is Jack's boss and the father of his girlfriend, but no one is dying." So the idea of returning to a Middle Eastern threat came back into play. Surnow continues, "We wanted to go back into the world we live in, which is more against radicalism. This season we decided to make it less superpower, James Bond, like the second season was. What we learned in season three is that the personal moments make the big terrorism stuff feel much more real. So let's go into the family of a sleeper cell: a mom, a dad, and a kid cooking breakfast and having orange juice and watching TV."

One of the most chilling aspects of the Araz family sleeper cell story was the idea that terrorists could be anyone in your neighborhood — an effective hook, but one that immediately garnered protests. "Fox promoted it as 'They could be next door to you' and that's what

got Muslims upset," Gordon explains. "When people found out about the family, they were afraid that this monolithic family were all terrorists." Cochran emphasises, "We didn't change the content of the show because we always intended for there to be some sense of balance with that. Of course, the Araz family seemingly being outwardly normal, that was a jarring thing for a lot of people, although I think it worked very well dramatically. But even within that family, we did not just set up three stereotypical 'terrorists'. One of them [Navi Araz] is unwaveringly stuck to the cause. One of them, the kid [Behrooz], decided it was too much when he saw someone die in front of him. He realized, 'I don't want to do this.' The third person, the mother [Dina], was caught in between. We treated them as three individuals who reacted with three very specific emotional and psychological ways to what was happening, and their family came undone because of it. So it may have started out looking like we were dealing with some sort of stereotypical thing, but I don't think we did. We have always had other characters who are Middle Eastern, but not terrorists. We have always been mindful of the need for balance."

Perhaps the biggest change introduced in season

four was the break in the story structure used in previous seasons. This year the writers just moved from one continuous threat to another and, to their surprise, the audience ate it up. Gordon laughs, "The theory was that it was an inconsistent season because it had everything but the kitchen sink. If you actually describe what happened, it's insane! Let's break down the Internet to facilitate melting down the nuclear power plants, which really was a slight of hand for the stealth bomber and a series of attacks with increasing improbability."

Cochran explains: "Before that season, we always thought we had to have an arc. We always felt like we had to have three big arcs that hold the season together, and that was the time when we realized that it was really okay as storytellers to have mini-arcs. There was a different thing in every episode or maybe it only lasts for a couple of episodes and then we are on to something else. As long as one thing leads to another in a way that is comprehensible and as long as the emotional or psychological state Jack is in is continuous, I think the audience liked having new problems each episode. So it was an eye-opener for us because we hadn't been thinking that way before, and when we ended up having to do that because that was the way the ideas came to us and it worked. It was freeing. It allowed us to improvise and be more spontaneous from week to week. We don't have to force ourselves to keep things in place.

Surnow thinks it also made something else very clear. "The real-time thing is not nearly as important, in terms of the reality and the logic of it, as the feel of making every hour count. It allows us to crank up each hour and make it a race. In terms of the reality of it, the audience doesn't care that you can't get anywhere in ten minutes in LA. They don't care about the absurd things. They just care that each hour is a cranked up, suspenseful hour and that's what we got from season four."

As the year wound down, there was almost an inevitability to the idea that Jack has to fake his death in order to escape the circumstances of the season. Gordon offers, "I think we were interested in reiterating the fact that Jack is really someone who can't escape his destiny, which on one hand is heroic and the other hand tragic." Cochran continues, "We again work out one of the themes of the show, which is that you can't do what he does or be who he is and have a satisfactory personal life.

This time we watched his personal life start in a good place with a woman that he loves and who loves him and unravel in various ways as his inability to stand back from the action causes him to jump back in and allows her to see sides to him that aren't wonderful. She's not used to it. It's not like she is an agent and sees this kind of thing all the time. It's scary and jarring for her. It's not like she suddenly stops loving him, but it does make her question whether a long-term relationship is viable. I think all of that was very organic to the story and the character. At the end, she expresses her doubts to him and it helps him decide it's time to 'die'. There was a story logic to it. Here is a guy who is willing to spend the rest of his life in jail if it suits his country – that's how loyal he is to the country. Then he is warned by a source he trusts that he's not even going to be permitted to do that. He's going to be killed in a devious way by somebody in the country he is trying to serve. Well, either he does allow himself to be killed or he has to escape somehow. Those are the only two choices he has. If he escapes, then the next season is about him being hunted and

that's not where the show lives. The alternative was for him to fake death so everyone thinks he is gone, which is a nice ending for the show."

In closing, Cochran offers, "I like season four. We did some over the top stuff but it all worked. Another thing we found out as we keep going is that because we have been to so many dark or weird places over the years, the audience will follow us to places that seem a little over the top. If you set it up right, the audience is watching Jack and as long as they don't say to themselves, 'How can he *do* that?' then we'd be in trouble. But if they see him do that and say, 'My God! He didn't have a choice!' or 'I don't know what I would do in that situation' then you are okay."

Surnow's perspective is similar. "I feel the same way about all the seasons — that there are a bunch of really, really good episodes and then there are a lot that are just functional and good. But with Jack, I think we've hit the notes that we want to hit. If you go too far it becomes bleak and you always want there to be a sense of hope for Jack."

Opposite: Kalil Hasan (Anil Kumar) gets to Andrew Paige (Lukas Haas) before Jack in season four.

Jack Bauer Returns: An Interview with Kiefer Sutherland

Two days. For average people, two days are most often just a blur of meaningless activity without serious accomplishment — non-distinctive tasks that become ticks in the figurative clock counting down their existence. But two days for Jack Bauer is something altogether different. As evidenced during the first two seasons of *24*, his forty-eight hours can be loaded with intense violence, destruction and heart-wrenching loss. These burdens rest heavily on Bauer's shoulders as he takes decisive action against enemies of the state, making decisions that will ultimately allow the rest of the world to blissfully spend their days without a care in the world.

In answering his call to duty to protect the country, over the four and a half years between season one and the beginning of season three Jack Bauer sacrifices more than most people can bear, with the brutal murder of his wife, Teri, and the resulting estrangement from his daughter, Kim. Yet for Kiefer Sutherland, Jack's journey has provided fertile ground for the actor to explore and develop the repercussions such tragedy has for a man so dedicated to service. Before *24*, Sutherland's television series experience was nil. But in just two seasons, the actor has embraced the unique opportunity the medium provides in crafting the character of Jack Bauer onscreen over years, rather than the limited few hours of a film.

Elevated to co-executive producer status at the beginning of season three, Sutherland worked closely with director Jon Cassar in the daily production of the show, helping to maintain the level of excellence set by the writers. In the trenches, working the dialogue with his fellow actors and always looking for the subtle nuances that bring the humanity of Bauer to the forefront, Sutherland says the focus of the third year was about making the real-time concept achieve everything it could onscreen. "It was a time when we were starting to realize the concept of a thriller and the visual excitement of the action really fusing together. We made a big effort to try and make that connect. Our concern, as much as broadening the show, was also maintaining the quality and the innovative things the writers were doing." Sutherland says, "We were all very aware of wanting to maintain that and it wasn't so much about always wanting to get better, but it was never wanting to do worse. From season to season, we have huge concerns about what we are doing all the way from scene to scene, and in some cases, line to line. Certain things work better and certain things don't. For the first two and half years, the storyline with my family was very difficult to maintain without it seeming very repetitious, and sometimes verging on silly. That was something we had to learn as we went and we were grateful for an audience willing to go with us on that. We will be the first to tell you that every year there have been things we have stumbled upon that were difficult for the writers to get around or were difficult for the actors to play. We make mistakes that we hope we will always be learning from, but for the most part, I think the writers have done a really fantastic job in every year moving forward from that."

The start of season three found Jack Bauer coming back from Mexico after a year of intense undercover work trying to bring down the Salazar drug cartel. As always, Bauer's dedication to the job meant he returned to CTU paying a price, enduring the effects of a heroin addiction. While it became the marquee storyline for the season and provided a compelling weakness for the writers to exploit, the physical limitations of the addiction proved to be difficult for Sutherland. "The real challenge is portraying a drug addiction in a twenty-

four hour period, and we really wanted to illustrate that he had one and it was something he had developed working undercover," the actor remembers. "The real trick is being able to figure out how in a twenty-four hour period to articulate a problem and deal with it in a way that is as realistic as possible, but then allow the character to move forward. Obviously, twenty-four hours is not a long period of time and so that can get creatively complicated from a reality perspective. But we worked to make those scenes work."

Critics and audiences lauded the gritty accuracy of Sutherland's withdrawal portrayal, and the actor admits he used his own life and personal experiences to shape Jack's pain. "I went to two doctors for research and, very unfortunately, I've had friends that have had problems in this area, one of who is very close to me and has been doing very well for ten years now. I spent a lot of time talking to that person as well." Physically draining and a hindrance to Bauer's stamina, the drug storyline eventually had to be phased out. "I don't think he could function as a normal person anymore, so he had to take other drugs that would allow him to go back

to being the Jack Bauer character that we know."

Providing his overall assessment of the third season, Sutherland says he was pleased in particular with the forward momentum of various characters' interpersonal relationships. "I think the storyline between Michelle Dessler and Tony Almeida started to develop well throughout that season. I loved working with [James] Badge Dale (Chase Edmunds). I thought he did an amazing job, like the stuff in the train station where he is trying to figure out what to do with his life. I thought [Elisha Cuthbert] did a fantastic job with it. I think certain fans were pre-disposed to have a problem with Kim, regardless, but I really did like the writing and what the writers did with her this year."

One of the seminal moments of the entire series came at the end of season three in the waning moments of the last episode. Sitting inside his truck, Bauer finally breaks down, sobbing as the weight of the day finally comes down upon his weary body and tortured psyche. A rare glimpse into Jack's soul, the depth of emotion in Sutherland's portrayal lingers long after the season fades to black. Remembering the day, the actor reveals, "It was something Jon and I were messing around with. We had this moment where the day was over and he was going to get into his car and go. We didn't really have a specific ending for Jack as well as we had, very clearly, an ending for the story for that year. We tried it a couple of times and I said to Jon, 'How far do you think we can go with this?' He said, 'Go as far as you want and we can pull back.' I said, 'I think he is on the verge of an absolute nervous breakdown right now at this stage with everything that's happened. The loss and the fear and everything he's had to hold in should really come out.' We tried it, and when I go into a moment like that I get a little lost. We finished it and I came out and pulled myself together and asked, 'What did you think?' Jon said, 'We got it. We're done.' So that's the kind of really special relationship I have with Jon Cassar. I trust him implicitly and he is absolutely there to encourage you to try and go as far as you can, and if it doesn't work he is there to tell you honestly. At least knowing from his perspective that he really liked that, it became the end and that's what we went with."

Unlike previous years, season three did not end

with a cliffhanger, which meant the writers were free to start season four with a clean slate. Audiences were shocked to find Jack Bauer happy, even smiling, content in his new job as a senior advisor for the Secretary of Defense and, more importantly, in love with Audrey Raines. It was a change of attitude that allowed Sutherland to open Bauer up and introduce a different side to the character. "It's impossible to continually follow a character that is starting from such a deep despair," Sutherland sighs. "You have to want him to get through the day for something and love is the greatest thing there is. If there is a love interest that an audience will buy, they have something to fight for and make life worth living for. The first three seasons were really dedicated to Jack's effort at maintaining his marriage and fixing that, and then dealing with

the loss of that opportunity, his wife, and the breaking of his family. It was time to put him back on much more solid ground. One of the reasons we continue pressing on in life is that there has to be this belief that around the corner, everything you ever dreamed of is there: love, happiness, challenges, the promise that you will find what you are supposed to do. And I wanted very much that this was an opportunity for Jack to have all those things. Audrey represented all of that. She was hope for Jack, and even through season five as well. I thought it was a nice arc."

Season four was also the year that the structure of the narrative progressed more aggressively than any year prior. Instead of three major arcs spread throughout the season, the writers created a stream of accelerating crises that barreled all the way through to the season

finale. While it was a risk, Sutherland says he wasn't surprised that audiences totally embraced it. "I've been amazed with it from the very beginning," he laughs softly. "I didn't think that audiences would accept the loss of my wife. As mad and as upset as they were in terms of emails and comments from people who watch the show, they applauded the fact that the writers were bold enough to do it. I'm amazed at the speed at which we relay information and go through plot points and how layered it is. This whole experience has been an amazing lesson for me on how savvy an audience is. There is little stuff that I would do character-wise for me, never expecting anyone to pick up on it and they all do. Little things like with the drug addiction and some very subtle stuff from the scratching of the arm to the slightest twitch or not being able to sit still in a scene, having to get up or sit down for no apparent reason at all. People

were picking up on stuff like that. There was one period where Kim Raver and I, whenever we would end a scene, whoever was the one to walk away, would walk away close enough to the other person so that they could touch hands. Many times it was off camera and you wouldn't see it. Jon caught it one day and started shooting it. It was really subtle in a really wide shot and audiences caught it."

While the producers select a main villain for every season, year four in particular drew intense fire for its depiction of a Muslim family as a terrorist cell. The producers reacted by working with Muslim rights groups to create public service announcements (PSAs) featuring Sutherland that denounced racism. But Sutherland says maintaining their creative integrity was just as important. "When I went and did a film like *A Time to Kill* and I played a Ku Klux Klan man, I wasn't supporting the Klan,

I was going to play a racist and showing this is the last guy you want to be. Any sixteen year-old kid that was using racism as a cop-out would see it and think, 'I don't want to be that guy,' so that was the intent for me doing that. The last thing in the world that we would want coming out of season four is someone to watch our show and think Muslims are bad or people from the Middle East are bad. At the same token, it would be absolutely ludicrous to pretend that a large proportion of terrorism is not coming out of the Middle East. It would be silly and irresponsible as well, so there's a balance. In that specific instance, the PSAs were helpful. And the American Muslim community and the organizations we have dealt with have been amazingly supportive in helping us find ways to tell stories that we want to tell but also create an awareness of why we are telling them.

"When you take an actress like Shohreh Aghdashloo [Dina Araz], she provided an amazing moment that I think made Jack really understand her character. People believe what they believe. People that feel they have been oppressed for hundreds of years and haven't been able to worship their religion as freely as they want to, they are going to have their beliefs and responses. Jack Bauer understood this with Dina and he also understood her as a parent. At some point, [regardless of] the different sides they may have been on ideologically about how to accomplish whatever they wanted to accomplish for their people, they find a common ground as parents and in the effort to save her son. He understood that and she understood that. It was one of those interesting moments where they could have been 180 degrees separated ideologically, yet they found a common ground

somewhere, and I think we need to figure that out in the real world too."

Reflecting on days three and four in Jack Bauer's life, Sutherland is still humbled by the success and stamina of this show that, according to naysayers, couldn't exist for more than a season. The actor says the key to understanding Jack, and partly also the enduring popularity of the show, is that he doesn't just endure, he evolves. "I think the character is still growing on many levels. Every season has impacted another, and the character has grown, and the character is allowed to carry with him what he has suffered the year before. The repercussions of his choices allow me as an actor to have an incredibly personal emotional response. I think the writers have done an amazing job giving us a balance. It was what I was originally attracted to in the pilot and it has been something that has been consistent to now."

Above: Hector (Vincent Laresca) and Ramon Salazar with Jack in season three.

Regular Cast:
Kiefer Sutherland (Jack Bauer)
Elisha Cuthbert (Kimberly Bauer)
Dennis Haysbert (President David Palmer)
Reiko Aylesworth (Michelle Dessler)
Carlos Bernard (Tony Almeida)
James Badge Dale (Chase Edmunds)

DAY THREE

1:00 pm - 2:00 pm

Director: Jon Cassar

Writers: Joel Surnow and Michael Loceff

Guest Cast: Lucinda Jenney (Helen Singer), DB Woodside (Wayne Palmer), Joaquim de Almeida (Ramon Salazar), Vincent Laresca (Hector Salazar)

"It's just going to be another one of those days."
President David Palmer

Timeframe	Key Events

1:00 P.M. In Los Angeles, a van pulls up to the NHS facility. A body is dropped off and a bomb is detonated.

1:02 P.M. Jack and his partner, Agent Chase Edmunds, face drug kingpin Ramon Salazar at a federal holding facility. Salazar stabs his lawyer in the throat with a pen.

1:08 P.M. At NHS, Dr Sunny Macer recognizes a strain of virus on the body. They alert CTU.

1:09 P.M. At CTU, Tony Almeida is warned by Macer that the body carries a pneumatic virus that might be a message from someone willing to unleash it.

1:12 P.M. Jack calls Tony, who warns him of the possible bio-threat.

1:14 P.M. President David Palmer meets his brother and Chief of Staff, Wayne, to prepare for a debate at the University of Southern California.

1:18 P.M. Tony and Michelle debate a move to Langley. Kim Bauer is working as a low-level analyst at CTU.

1:21 P.M. In northern Mexico, Ramon Salazar's brother Hector gets a call about the body.

1:25 P.M. At CTU, Jack snaps at his coordinator Chloe O'Brian and goes into his office.

1:27 P.M. Chase finds Kim in a back room and they kiss. Kim wants to tell her dad about their relationship.

1:29 P.M. Macer informs CTU that the virus has been engineered to kill more rapidly, as many as one million people in a week.

1:30 P.M. Kyle, a teen in Canoga Park, hides a bag of drugs in his room.

1:38 P.M. Tony gets an anonymous call demanding the release of Ramon in six hours or the virus will be released. The body is IDd as a drug dealer from East LA.

1:48 P.M. Wayne alerts Palmer about the viral threat.

1:52 P.M. Jack sequesters himself in his office and prepares to inject himself with heroin. A call from Kim stops him.

Salazar stabs his lawyer.

Chase and Kim share a moment.

Jack on the brink.

The opening of season three found Jack Bauer in the most shocking of circumstances, addicted to heroin after working undercover for months trying to bust the Salazar drug cartel in Mexico. The hero of the story was now in the extremely vulnerable position of jeopardizing his job and his own life due to his secret. Co-executive producer and director Jon Cassar explains their approach in portraying this new facet of the character. "One of the most interesting years for both Kiefer and I was when he had to play the drug addiction. It gave the whole series a new twist and a new challenge, but you have to rise to the occasion because it's going to be harder than usual. Jack Bauer isn't going to be the usual Jack Bauer and we have to oversee him in a different way. Everything he does needs to be approached differently: when he's in the field, when he's talking to his daughter or his colleagues at CTU. I think both Kiefer

Research Files

Biological Terrorism: The main threat of season three revolves around the release of a fictitious immuno pulmonary virus in the United States. In reality, the human release of a natural or human-manufactured toxin or 'bio-agent' is a relatively new threat to the world populace. Strides in science have allowed for the isolation of toxic agents, such as smallpox, anthrax, botulin, and ebola, so they can be disseminated with variable control on selected populations. While bioterrorists can not control who will contract the disease or be immune to it, they can be guaranteed, based on the communicability and toxicity of the release, that large groups of people will be affected and in turn continue to infect others until containment. One of the best examples of recent bioterrorism occurred in 2001, with the anthrax attacks on Washington DC shortly after 9/11

and I do everything we can not to hold back. Our job is to push it as far as we can and we were both in agreement on trying to show the addiction as close to reality as we could. We didn't want the freaked out, movie version. We wanted it to be the quiet need for the drugs. The way we dealt with him was that everything became a little more heightened. It was Jack Bauer with a little more attitude and a little more impatience — if you can believe that Jack Bauer could be more impatient than he is already! It was reflected in the action. The action was a little more violent and a little more raw. Everything he did was based on the fact that he was fighting his drug addiction and that really became the nucleus for Jack Bauer for the year."

Additional Intel

The third season première of *24* aired commercial-free for the first time ever in North America. The episode ran fifty-one minutes and in repeats was edited down to forty-three minutes. The première was sponsored by Ford Motor Company, who produced a two-part commercial that ran before and after the episode, and was an homage to the series.

2:00 pm - 3:00 pm

Director: Jon Cassar

Writers: Joel Surnow and Michael Loceff

Guest Cast: Vanessa Ferlito (Claudia Salazar), Christina Chang (Dr Sunny Macer), Wendy Crewson (Anne Packard), Joaquim de Almeida (Ramon Salazar)

"Shut up, stupid! You just fired at a federal agent. You better start talking to me, or I will let you bleed to death right here on this landing." Jack Bauer

Timeframe

2:00 P.M. Jack puts the heroin vial back in his medical bag.

2:02 P.M. Tony briefs Wayne about the threat. Wayne reiterates Palmer's policy of not negotiating with terrorists.

2:05 P.M. Kim calls Jack and asks to speak with him. Chase suggests Jack go on methadone to help his addiction, but Jack refuses.

2:07 P.M. Kim tells Jack about her relationship with Chase and he is unhappy.

2:11 P.M. Macer alerts Michelle Dessler at CTU that the virus is in crystalline form, like cocaine.

2:12 P.M. Kyle is ordered to drop the drugs off.

2:20 P.M. Palmer questions if the debate should go on with the viral threat. Wayne disagrees and Senator Keeler arrives.

2:22 P.M. Chase and Jack have a heated discussion about Kim.

2:30 P.M. Wayne updates Palmer and reveals he may have access to Keeler's debate playbook.

2:35 P.M. Hector Salazar has a fight with his girlfriend Claudia.

2:38 P.M. Jack and Chase arrive at a crack den where the drug dealer worked. They enter without backup.

2:43 P.M. Jack gets one of Salazar's low level flunkies to admit that a drug mule named Kyle has an expensive bag of cocaine Salazar wants.

2:46 P.M. Kyle's girlfriend finds the bag of cocaine.

2:55 P.M. Palmer talks to his girlfriend/personal physician, Anne, about the virus threat.

2:57 P.M. Jack goes after Kyle and sends Chase back to CTU in order to protect him.

2:58 P.M. Wayne shows Palmer Keeler's playbook which holds damaging information about Anne.

2:59 P.M. Salazar's informant, Gael, is revealed as a CTU employee.

Key Events

Keeler and Palmer at the debate.

Hector hits Claudia.

Gael is Hector's mole.

Kim Bauer has always been one of the most vexing characters on *24*. Impatient fans grew weary of Kim being in constant peril over two seasons, and this made it a challenge for the writers to win back audience sympathy. In season three, the producers made a conscious decision to have Kim more integrated into the storyline by making her a low-level analyst at CTU. Frustrated herself with the character over the years, actress Elisha Cuthbert admits that she was much more satisfied with this change. "Season three was so strong for Kim. It was a big year for her." But Cuthbert was still uncertain about returning for the year, "It was a big conversation with the producers, hours and

hours before going back into it. I was saying, 'I'm not coming back to be put back in the situations that she was put in. If Kim is going to return, either don't have her at all or have her doing something proactive as opposed to reactive.' That was the real problem with season two. She was just sitting there and dealing when she should have been doing something. But putting her in CTU this season put her in real conflict, with the dynamic between her and her dad and the people in CTU, with all the talk that she just got the job because of her dad. There were real problems and not just these false things thrown in."

Kim was also given a grown-up relationship with Chase Edmunds, Jack's partner. Of the romance, Cuthbert says, "I liked it and thought it was smart. It meant Jack got stuck in the middle of it all and I think it made sense. It's also very real for two people in the work environment to start a relationship. It made for some really exciting moments on the show."

Research Files

Methadone: One of the biggest shocks of season three is the revelation that Jack Bauer became addicted to heroin while working undercover to bust the Salazar drug cartel. Jack's partner, Chase Edmunds, is aware of Jack's problem and tries to get him on methadone to quit. Methadone is a synthetic opioid introduced to the United States in 1947 by pharmaceutical company Eli Lilly. It is a strong analgesic and was found to be particularly effective for people suffering the intense side effects of heroin addiction. The ingestion of methadone cuts an addict's appetite for heroin, which assists in the rehabilitation process. Due to the addictive nature of methadone itself, the administering of the drug is usually undertaken at a methadone maintenance clinic, where medical professionals can monitor the entire process, ensuring the best chances of success for the patient.

Additional Intel

Unlike previous seasons, where the first scene of the season occurs in a foreign country, season three is the first year to have the action begin in the United States, specifically outside of Los Angeles, California.

3:00 pm - 4:00 pm

Director: Ian Toynton
Writer: Howard Gordon

Guest Cast: Christina Chang (Dr Sunny Macer), Wendy Crewson (Anne Packard), Joaquim de Almeida (Ramon Salazar), Vanessa Ferlito (Claudia Salazar)

"The virus is out!" Jack Bauer

Timeframe	Key Events

3:00 P.M. Dr Nicole Duncan, the head of Health Services, arrives at Jack's car with a Hazmat team to assist him at Kyle's. She sees his heroin on the floor.

3:05 P.M. Michelle enlists Gael's aid in sourcing the terrorist call.

3:06 P.M. Gael calls Hector to alert him about Jack closing in on the virus.

3:09 P.M. Kyle and his father fight. His duffel bag rips open and the cocaine bag is broken open in the apartment.

3:18 P.M. Salazar summons the District Attorney to his cell to talk.

3:19 P.M. Palmer refuses to believe the allegations about Anne, but Wayne encourages him to confront Anne before the debate.

3:20 P.M. Salazar's guard kills the District Attorney.

3:22 P.M. CTU forcibly enters Kyle's house. His parents panic and dump the cocaine down the toilet. Jack alerts Tony the virus is in the sewage system and may be airborne.

3:28 P.M. Palmer confronts Anne. Her ex-husband is accusing her of lying about her knowledge of his fabricated drug research. She denies it and David believes her. Wayne asks David to meet him.

3:30 P.M. Macer tells Tony she believes they can contain the virus.

3:32 P.M. Duncan determines the powder is safe but theorizes that Kyle is a human host carrying the virus.

3:41 P.M. Wayne tells Palmer that Anne's ex wants money, which at Wayne's prompting, he agrees to pay.

3:45 P.M. Kyle's dad calls his son, who thinks his parents ratted him out, and he hangs up. Tony is able to trace his location.

3:53 P.M. Chase is angry about being shut out of the case by Jack.

3:55 P.M. Duncan confronts Jack about his addiction. He admits he became addicted while undercover with the Salazars.

3:59 P.M. Salazar's man, Gomez, and Tony find Kyle. Gomez shoots Tony in the neck and Kyle runs.

Salazar gets his revenge on the DA.

The cocaine goes down the toilet.

Tony is shot down.

Casting new characters each season is the challenge for Emmy award-winning *24* casting gurus Debi Manwiller and Peggy Kennedy. One of the more difficult roles to cast for season three was Chase Edmunds. Casting director Manwiller remembers, "We auditioned a lot of people. Badge was someone we were aware of, but I hadn't seen his audition tapes or met him in person. There was a lot of buzz about him. It was a really hard role to cast because we were trying to find someone to match with Elisha [Cuthbert], who is younger, but also find someone who was supposed to work closely with Kiefer. We were trying to figure out what the relationship

between him and Kiefer was going to be — was Kiefer more of a mentor or was Chase more of a peer? Part of it was going to be told in casting, because if we had cast someone older, it would have been less of a mentor and more of a peer." Peggy Kennedy adds, "Later they threw in that Chase was going to be a love interest for Kim." Manwiller sighs adding, "It made it so much harder because he essentially had the same job as Jack, but was working under him. Kiefer's so powerful that you have to find someone to match him as an actor and someone people believe that Jack Bauer respects enough to take along with him. We got James Badge Dale's tape pretty far into the process. He was in a play at the time and he had tested for a feature film that he was close to getting." Kennedy explains, "He tested for us and literally, he walked out of the room and we said, 'We want him.' After us, he went in to meet with the movie people. It was really crazy." Dale decided to take 24 and the rest is history. Manwiller smiles, "There were some moments when we thought we might not get him and we were really close to shooting. It was down to the wire!"

Research Files

Los Angeles County Department of Health Services: When the viral threat is determined, the head of DHS, Dr Nicole Duncan, becomes part of Jack's team in stopping the outbreak from becoming a pandemic. In reality, DHS of Los Angeles is truly responsible for providing public and personal health services to the ten million residents of the county. DHS operates four major hospitals in Los Angeles and provides public health programs including bioterrorism prevention. In the case of a viral outbreak, DHS would alert citizens how to protect themselves through the media and on their website, which gives an exhaustive list of types of agents, symptoms to look out for and ways to protect yourself from infection.

Additional Intel

Kiefer Sutherland won his first Screen Actor's Guild Award for Outstanding Performance by a Male Actor in a Drama Series for season three.

4:00 pm - 5:00 pm

Director: Ian Toynton
Writer: Stephen Kronish

Guest Cast: Riley Smith (Kyle Singer), Andrea Thompson (Nicole Duncan), DB Woodside (Wayne Palmer), Jesse Borrego (Gael Ortega)

"Sometimes you have to do the wrong thing for the right reasons." President David Palmer

Timeframe / Key Events

4:00 P.M. Jack calls Michelle about Tony. She is in command of CTU.

4:05 P.M. Kyle's girlfriend picks him up; Gomez follows them.

4:06 P.M. Chase leaves to interrogate Salazar again.

4:12 P.M. Jack calls Palmer to alert him they won't get Kyle before the virus is released. Wayne briefs the President on quarantine and evacuation procedures.

4:15 P.M. Kyle admits he may have contracted a disease in Mexico. His girlfriend wants out of the car and when they pull over Gomez kidnaps them both.

4:18 P.M. Jack poses a plan to the President where he breaks Salazar out of prison so that CTU thinks Jack has switched sides. He gets the President to approve the plan.

4:24 P.M. Anne confronts Wayne about his secretive actions.

4:25 P.M. Chloe catches Gael receiving a personal phone call on his cell, which is against protocol.

4:27 P.M. Hector expresses his frustration to Gael. Hanging up, he then teaches Claudia's little brother to fire a gun. She is livid and aims a gun at Hector without shooting.

4:31 P.M. Anne gets David to admit to paying the blackmail.

4:33 P.M. Palmer calls Wayne and orders him not to pay the ex.

4:41 P.M. Jack calls Kim and walks her through generating a prisoner transfer document for Salazar. He finds out Chase is going to see Salazar.

4:44 P.M. Chase gets into Salazar's cell and brutally attacks him.

4:50 P.M. Jack arrives and attacks Chase to Salazar's surprise. Jack informs him that he will be set free and they tie up Chase.

4:42 P.M. Wayne confronts Anne and threatens her.

4:54 P.M. Jack walks out with Salazar and the warden lets them through.

4:56 P.M. The warden finds Chase and he sets off the alarm. Jack forces a guard at gunpoint to open all the cells, releasing all the prisoners.

Gomez catches Kyle's girlfriend.

Anne faces Wayne down.

Jack's desperate action.

Playing the vicious Ramon Salazar behind bars in the initial episodes of the season, actor Joaquim de Almeida says that the format and organic writing process of the series made it hard for him to figure out the motivations of his character. "I remember talking to Joel [Surnow] and saying, 'Listen, I am sensing that I am playing towards something but I don't know what I am talking about because you don't give me any more than two scripts at a time and I need to know what the hell I am talking about!'" he laughs. "So they would give me hints. They said, 'Okay, at a certain point, but we don't know when... you are going to get out of prison.' So I said, 'Okay, now

I know I am getting out of prison!' Then when we were talking about that scene they said, 'Well, when you get out of prison make sure you get dressed, because once we start shooting nights, it's going to get really cold out there in the desert.' It was really strange to work that way, because when you do a film, you know the beginning, the middle and the end. It was challenging to read a script every time. But my character always had exciting physical and emotional scenes. Like I finally figured out that Kiefer's character had lived with me for a while and got addicted to drugs. When I read that I went, 'That's new!' I had no idea what I was talking about in the first speech, when I was talking to Jack right before I killed the lawyer on the first day of shooting. I had no idea and then I read that and figured, 'Oh, *that's* what I was talking about! Now I know!'"

Research Files

Federal Bureau of Prisons: The prison holding Ramon Salazar in the opening episodes of Day Three is a Federal detention center maintained by the Federal Bureau of Prisons (FBP). Criminals that perpetrate crimes against the United States or violate laws on a Federal level are incarcerated in Federal prisons. A subdivision of the United States Department of Justice, the FBP was established in 1930 to oversee the proper care of inmates. The bureau maintains more than 106 institutions with an excess of 180,000 Federal offenders at any given time. Federal executions are administered through the Bureau at the federal lethal injection chamber in Terre Haute, Indiana.

Additional Intel

Joaquim de Almeida is a world-renowned actor from Portugal. He speaks six languages: Portuguese, English, Spanish, French, Italian and German. He became a US citizen in 2005.

5:00 pm – 6:00 pm

Director: Jon Cassar
Writer: Evan Katz

Guest Cast: Wendy Crewson (Anne Packard), Joaquim de Almeida (Ramon Salazar), Vanessa Ferlito (Claudia Salazar), Vincent Laresca (Hector Salazar)

"Congratulations! Now you are an even bigger enemy to your country than I am." Ramon Salazar

Timeframe	Key Events

5:02 P.M. Amongst a prison riot, Jack and Salazar knock out two guards and don their uniforms.

5:05 P.M. Chase informs the warden of the virus threat. Chase tells Michelle Jack freed Salazar.

5:08 P.M. Kim identifies Kyle on a traffic cam and Michelle informs Kim of her father's actions.

5:09 P.M. Jack and Salazar are taken hostage by rioting prisoners.

5:16 P.M. Kyle attempts suicide so the virus will die with him, but he fails.

5:18 P.M. Gael calls Hector about CTU being close to finding Kyle.

5:19 P.M. Kim identifies that someone has Kyle at gunpoint and attempts to ID the truck.

5:20 P.M. A ruthless inmate named Peel forces Jack and another guard to play Russian Roulette for their lives. The guard pulls the trigger and dies.

5:29 P.M. Kim waits for an image of the truck to download but the router fails.

5:30 P.M. Gael scrambles to stop the download.

5:32 P.M. Michelle calls on Tony's condition and gets a feed of his surgery, which upsets her.

5:34 P.M. Chase arranges explosives around the prison perimeter.

5:35 P.M. Peel forces Salazar and Jack to play another round of Russian Roulette. They both fire but no rounds are loaded.

5:37 P.M. Jack shoots Peel and Chase is able to blast into their room. Jack and Salazar run to the door.

5:43 P.M. Chloe finds Jack's drug kit in the trash.

5:44 P.M. At the debate, Keeler accuses Anne of lying about drug trial results.

5:48 P.M. Chloe reveals Jack's heroin to Kim and Michelle. The truck with Kyle is located and Michelle orders a raid.

5:55 P.M. Jack demands use of the CTU helicopter from Chase, who relents.

5:58 P.M. CTU rescues Kyle and his girlfriend.

5:59 P.M. Chase attempts to tell Jack about Kyle but Jack can't hear him. He and Salazar take off.

Kyle tries to hang himself.

Jack plays Russian Roulette.

Chloe finds Jack's secret.

The introduction of Chloe O'Brian this season was a huge departure from the typical analysts seen lurking about CTU for the past three seasons. Abrasive and a little bit weird, Chloe was the brainchild of executive producer Joel Surnow. "The way it worked with Chloe was that I saw Mary Lynn [Rajskub] in *Punch-Drunk Love* and I loved her," he enthuses. "I loved her character. I thought, 'You know, she's funny but there's something edgy about her and it might work here.' Obviously, if it were a silly character, it wouldn't do. She's like a female Napoleon Dynamite."

While Surnow was relatively confident about what the character

would bring to the mix, others weren't so sure. Executive producer Evan Katz remembers, "I have to say when Joel came up with the idea for Chloe, I was really not convinced that this would work... but I was proven very wrong. She just seemed too comedic for a show that we had tried really hard to make not comedic. The same goes for Edgar [Stiles]. I was worried these people seemed relatively incompetent and what the hell were they doing working in CTU? But people bought it and enjoyed it. I think the truth is that the audience recognized in them people who they worked with. Everyone has a semi-autistic, socially inept person in their midst who is very good at what they do, but is terrible at relating to people, and for that reason it worked." Evans now considers her one of his favorites to write for, "Chloe is the most fun because there is a lot of personality to her. It's not generally a show where you got to write good or snappy lines for your characters. We try to make sure the writing doesn't call attention to itself as much as possible, but with Chloe you can be a smart ass."

Research Files

Russian Roulette: The sick 'game' Jack and Salazar are forced to play by Peel is called Russian Roulette. Typically, the twisted pastime refers to the process of loading one bullet into the chamber of a revolver, spinning the cylinder, then pointing the gun at one's head and pulling the trigger. The odds of surviving the game are determined by the number of bullets put into the chambers. While the exact origins of the suicidal practice are unknown, two anecdotes that originated in Russia suggest possible sources. One involves prisoners who were forced to play for the amusement of their guards who then bet on the outcome. The other story describes suicidal Russian soldiers developing the practice while in despair. One of the most famous Russian Roulette scenes portrayed on film is a scene featuring actor Christopher Walken in *The Deer Hunter*.

Additional Intel

Due to the highly controversial depiction of Jack and Salazar being forced into a game of Russian Roulette, Kiefer Sutherland recorded a voiceover public service announcement, in conjunction with the Americans For Gun Safety Foundation, that ran after the episode, addressing the issue of gun safety.

6:00 pm - 7:00 pm

Director: Jon Cassar
Writer: Duppy Demetrius

Guest Cast: Jesse Borrego (Gael Ortega), Wendy Crewson (Anne Packard), Paul Schulze (Ryan Chappelle), Zachary Quinto (Adam Kaufman)

"We accepted you; you didn't have to put a needle in your arm. You did that for other reasons, same reason as all junkies, to kill the pain. What's your pain Jack?" Ramon Salazar

Timeframe	Key Events

6:00 P.M. Jack pilots the helicopter into downtown LA.

6:01 P.M. District Director Ryan Chappelle takes over control of CTU. He orders the military to shoot down Jack.

6:03 P.M. Chappelle says that Jack is now expendable.

6:06 P.M. Michelle suggests that Kim remove herself from the job until the situation with Jack is handled, but Kim refuses.

6:08 P.M. Chase calls Chappelle and recommends that he talk to President Palmer before shooting Jack down.

6:09 P.M. Chappelle calls Wayne with an update on the virus and Jack.

6:10 P.M. Wayne alerts Palmer of the situation in his earpiece and the President ends the debate blaming a national security emergency.

6:18 P.M. A frightened Kyle and his girlfriend are put under Dr Duncan's care at NHS.

6:20 P.M. The military locks onto Jack awaiting the order to fire. Chloe frantically tries to contact Jack.

6:21 P.M. Palmer balks at firing at Jack, but Wayne says getting rid of Salazar is more important. Palmer gives the order to fire.

6:24 P.M. Jack eludes the military among the tall buildings and lands on the street below. Jack and Salazar run.

6:30 P.M. Kyle's parents arrive and they share a tearful good-bye with their son.

6:37 P.M. Jack and Salazar take a car from a valet parking lot.

6:41 P.M. Wayne urges Palmer to denounce Jack.

6:45 P.M. Michelle is alerted that Tony will recover.

6:52 P.M. Palmer suffers in the post debate polls and Anne suggests they separate, but he refuses.

6:55 P.M. Duncan tells Kyle he is not infected.

6:57 P.M. Jack arrives at an airstrip and Salazar's men take him prisoner. Hector calls and tells Ramon to bring Jack to him alive.

6:59 P.M. Kim stumbles upon Gael's video feed of Jack. He comes into the room with a gun.

Palmer stops the debate.

Jack lands in downtown LA.

Salazar takes Jack to Mexico.

In season three, veteran film and television director Brad Turner was invited by Joel Surnow to direct episodes 9:00 pm – 10:00 pm and 10:00 pm – 11:00 pm. Having worked with Surnow on the series *La Femme Nikita*, Turner was pleased to get the opportunity to work with him again. "I have been a visiting director for a long time, with *Alias*, *Las Vegas* and *Battlestar Galactica*," Turner explains. "So you tend to adapt to where you go and how they do things. If anything, *24* is an easier show for me to adapt to because I'm used to doing my own movies and miniseries and this is very much a filmmakers' television series. Joel writes, produces and posts the shows, but he really needs the

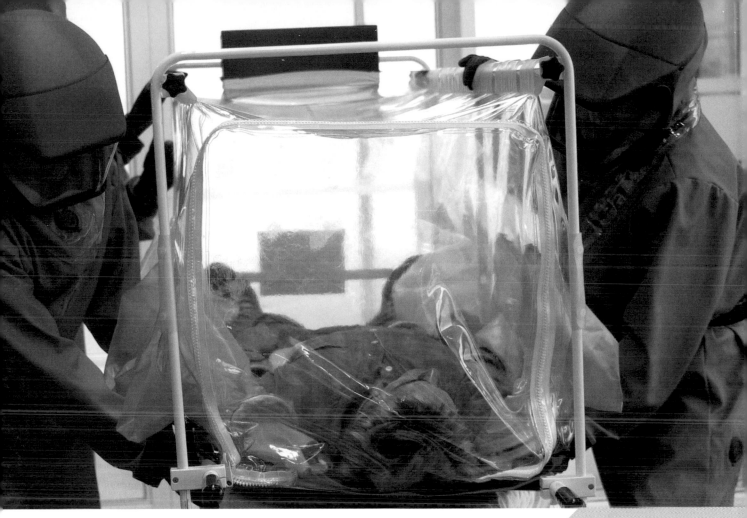

directors to go off and make the film for him. Both Jon [Cassar] and I feel like filmmakers doing this show. We have the freedom to direct the actors the way we want. Our free form style allows us to tell the story in many different ways because of how we move the camera. A lot of the things you are taught in film school you can throw out in this series because the sense that we are catching something happening in real time allows you to be more free form and not locked down to the language of film in a traditional sense. It also works with the acting style. We allow the characters more room to move. In a lot of ways, it's terrifying for the new cast members because it's not, 'Here's your close-up and then we will get a shot of you walking saying that line.' We do that all in one, and often we combine two or three scenes together, so it always feels to the audience that the camera is just getting there for the moment. It isn't anticipating anything. In a lot of ways, it's a breath of fresh air. From the audience point of view, the sense is that it's more complicated than normal, when in fact I think the reverse is true."

Research Files

No Fly Zone: Jack flies the helicopter right through downtown Los Angeles, which is not allowed in the United States without permission from the Federal Aviation Administration. No Fly Zones are areas designated domestically or internationally which, to maintain the safety of the citizens or territory below, unauthorized aircraft are not allowed to fly over. In this episode, the military does not shoot down Jack's helicopter due to the proximity to highly populated buildings and citizens below. In official instances where a No Fly Zone is in place, like the airspace over the White House, and a violation is committed, the military is mandated to shoot the aircraft down after a clear warning.

Additional Intel

Actress Alberta Watson, who played Erin Driscoll, first worked with Joel Surnow and Bob Cochran when they cast her as Madeline on the series *La Femme Nikita*. Ironically, her name was the basis for the season one character Alberta Green, played by Tamara Tunie.

Kim Bauer

Experience:

CTU – Level One Analyst, Los Angeles Domestic Unit

Education:

Santa Monica College – Associate of Arts, Computer
Programming

GED Certificate

Santa Monica High School – Dropped out before
matriculation

Personal:

Parents – Jack Bauer and Teri Bauer (deceased)

Chase Edmunds

CTU Missions:

All undercover operations – security clearance required for viewing records

Experience:

CTU – Field Operations Agent, Los Angeles Domestic Unit

CTU – Field Operations Agent, Washington/Baltimore Domestic Unit, Washington DC

MPD – Emergency Response Team (SWAT)

Awards:

Honors in Tactical Shooting – MPDC SWAT competition

Commendations in Weapons and Field Reconnaissance

Education:

Washington DC MPD – ERT basic training

Washington DC MPD – Police Academy Special Forces Operations Training Course

Personal:

Single

7:00 pm - 8:00 pm

Director: Ian Toynton
Writers: Robert Cochran & Howard Gordon

Guest Cast: DB Woodside (Wayne Palmer), Paul Schulze (Ryan Chappelle), Zachary Quinto (Adam Kaufman), Mary Lynn Rajskub (Chloe O'Brian)

> "Look Michelle, if I ever need you to trust me, it's now."
> Tony Almeida

Timeframe   Key Events

7:00 P.M. Gael duct tapes Kim to a chair and deletes the Salazar files.

7:03 P.M. Michelle tells Adam she is going to be with Tony and puts Gael in charge.

7:05 P.M. With Kyle clean, Chappelle alerts CTU that getting Salazar back is the priority.

7:08 P.M. Chappelle orders Chase back to CTU.

7:09 P.M. Adam searches for Kim but Gael says she was re-assigned.

7:11 P.M. Adam gets Michelle to override the access codes so he can enter the locked room. He finds Kim, alerts security and they catch Gael before he escapes.

7:20 P.M. Michelle leaves and Chappelle handles the Gael interrogation.

7:22 P.M. Ramon wants to kill Jack, but Hector's henchman convinces him to wait.

7:24 P.M. Jack fakes drug withdrawal symptoms and manages to overcome his guard and get his gun.

7:30 P.M. White House Press Secretary Gerry Whitehorn suggests Palmer distance himself from Anne.

7:31 P.M. Anne gets a call from her ex who wants to see her and she agrees.

7:34 P.M. Ramon is captured at gunpoint by Jack.

7:36 P.M. Hector awaits the plane with his soldiers.

7:37 P.M. Chappelle's torture elicits nothing from Gael, but when his cell rings, they force him to answer to Hector. They can't get a trace.

7:43 P.M. Michelle sees Tony and he insists on returning to CTU.

7:46 P.M. Chase calls Kim and tells her he is going dark to track down Jack in Mexico.

7:54 P.M. Tony returns to CTU and orders Chappelle to leave Gael alone.

7:56 P.M. Hector greets Jack with a hug to Ramon's confusion.

7:59 P.M. Gael and Tony reveal their plan to get Jack back in with the Salazars. Tony calls Palmer.

Jack turns the tables on Salazar.

Tony wants out of the hospital.

Hector embraces Jack.

Casting director Debi Manwiller says that the character of Claudia Salazar, Hector's wife, presented a particular problem for the casting and the writers just before mid-season. After a long search, they narrowed it down to two actresses "Eva Longoria [*Desperate Housewives*] came in and she was our second choice, but we decided to go with Vanessa Ferlito. They talked about Claudia maybe having been an agent before with Jack. The storyline was that she and Jack had known each other, but the writers weren't sure how. At one point they discussed the idea that they had worked together undercover, not just that they had had a relationship in the past, and she was an agent. It was an

ongoing process during casting so we didn't know how it was going to work out."

Since many of the secondary characters aren't contracted for a full season, the actors are able to audition and sign up for other projects during filming. That means the writers risk losing a character if there are shooting conflicts for the actor. Vanessa Ferlito was a perfect example of this. Casting associate Peggy Kennedy reveals, "We had to kill her. We would have gone on with her, at least until episode thirteen. However, we lost her by episode ten because she got a movie [*Man of the House*]." Manwiller adds, "We definitely didn't plan on killing her. We have so many people that aren't series regulars and they all come in and out the door. She was probably the worst example of where they had to change a major part of their storyline. We kill actors after we get them here, but she was the first one we actually *had* to kill because she was unavailable."

Research Files

Mexican Drug Cartels: The Salazar brothers are the leaders of a powerful drug cartel located in Las Nieves, Mexico. Illegal drug trafficking is a massive black market industry that deals with the production, packaging, distribution and sale of narcotics throughout the world. Mexico is a big player in the drug distribution chain with the US/Mexican border being one of the biggest gateways to bring illegal substances into the United States. Mexican cartels are usually the distributors of drugs that are grown and processed by the most powerful cartels located in Central America. The drugs most often distributed through cartels include heroin, cannabis, meth-amphetamines, opium and LSD. One of the most notorious Mexican cartels was the Ochoa brothers, who were members of the infamous Medellín cartel of Columbia.

Additional Intel

Writer/producer Evan Katz won the Writer's Guild of America Best Episodic Drama award for this episode. It is the only episode of *24* to be nominated or win a WGA in its history.

8:00 pm - 9:00 pm

Director: Ian Toynton
Writer: Robert Cochran & Howard Gordon

Guest Cast: Julian Rodriguez (Sergio), Greg Ellis (Michael Amador), Zachary Quinto (Adam Kaufman), Wendy Crewson (Anne Packard)

"I'm tired of putting my ass on the line for nothing. I'm done putting my ass on the line for nothing." Jack Bauer

Timeframe   Key Events

8:00 P.M. Tony calls the President to explain that it was all an elaborate ruse to smoke out a more dangerous group of Ukrainian scientists selling a weaponized virus. A pre-recorded message from Jack explains further.

8:05 P.M. Palmer is angry with Tony, but agrees to allow military help for the Mexican meeting.

8:06 P.M. CTU is up in arms at the revelation, with Michelle distrustful of Tony and Chappelle angry.

8:07 P.M. Hector explains to Ramon that Jack has set them up to make millions by reselling the virus to Korea or Al Qaeda operatives. Ramon is still suspicious and aims a gun at Jack, which Hector swats away.

8:15 P.M. Kim alerts Tony that Chase going dark may blow Jack's cover.

8:16 P.M. Jack suffers withdrawal and Claudia admonishes him for not revealing to her that he is a cop.

8:20 P.M. Tony tells Kim and Michelle that he is sending Rafael Gutierrez in to stop Chase.

8:21 P.M. Palmer tells Wayne he is worried he can't contact Anne.

8:22 P.M. Anne meets her ex-husband and is horrified when he commits suicide in front of her.

8:32 P.M. Anne calls Palmer and explains the letters exonerating her. Wayne is pleased.

8:44 P.M. Chase holds Gutierrez at gunpoint. Gutierrez puts Chase on the phone with Tony, but is shot dead. Chase is taken by snipers while CTU listens.

8:51 P.M. Anne ends her relationship with Palmer.

8:55 P.M. Jack calls the Ukrainian contact, Michael Amador. Chase is brought in and amid the chaos, Jack's locator watch is smashed. Hector demands Jack shoot Chase to prove what side he is on, he does — but there is no bullet.

8:59 P.M. Jack tells Chase to keep quiet.

Anne wrestles with her ex-husband.

Palmer and Anne say goodbye.

The Salazars test Jack.

The middle of the season meant more hard times for Chase Edmunds. Following Jack out to Mexico to try and help/stop him turned into a whole lot of pain and torture for the young agent. Grabbed by the Salazars, Edmunds spends the next few episodes being brutally beaten in a barn. James Badge Dale remembers those scenes being very difficult to shoot. "It was very uncomfortable. We just went at it. We were in splits all the time, which means we were shooting basically all night. We were about twenty miles north of Los Angeles on a little reserve place and it was barren. It was really cold at night and we were literally in a shack on this property in the middle of

nowhere. They weren't exactly sure what they were going to do or how they were going to do it, so we had to play around and do a lot of different things to see how it came together. Michael Geiger [the weapons expert] was there holding a rope and stringing me up. Then they would say 'Cut!' he'd let me down for a little bit, and then bring me back up. I've never done anything like that in my life and if I *never* have to do anything like that again, I'll be okay," he laughs. "I think we pushed it a bit, especially when it gets to six am and everybody has been working all night. It has been twelve hours and we still have to beat the crap out of me. Attitudes start to show, tensions get raised, and when you see that, you have to calm everyone down and take it easy. It was tough but they did a wonderful job."

Research Files

Transponders: Jack's watch is fitted with a transponder that allows CTU to track his location in Mexico. After a skirmish, the watch is cracked and the transponder is disabled. In real life, Radio Frequency Identification (RFID) is a method that works with tags or transponders. There are tag or chip-based RFID tags that allow for the tracking of items, devices or people. There are three types of tags known as passive, semi-active, and active. Passive tags have no internal power supply and can be read from a distance of four inches to several meters. Active tags have their own power supply, can be read from distances up to 300 feet, and store information sent by the transceiver. Tags are getting smaller and smaller and in the future all humans may be fitted with tags that will allow for tracking, which would be helpful in cases of missing people, or disturbing if used to infringe on personal or privacy rights.

Additional Intel

Director Jon Cassar reveals that the writers invented the pill that Jack Bauer is given by the Salazars to quench his heroin addiction because no such pill exists.

9:00 pm – 10:00 pm

Director: Brad Turner
Writers: Robert Cochran & Howard Gordon
Teleplay: Evan Katz & Stephen Kronish

Guest Cast: Josh Cruz (Oriol), Jamie McShane (Gerry Whitehorn), Gina Torres (Julia Milliken), Sarah Clarke (Nina Myers)

"The man has more lives than a cat."
Ramon Salazar

Timeframe	Key Events

9:00 P.M. Palmer faces the press about the abrupt end to the debate.

9:02 P.M. Tony and CTU try to reestablish a link with Jack's transponder.

9:04 P.M. Amador calls and will only talk to Jack. He instructs him to meet them in 15 minutes. Salazar sees Jack is in a bad state of withdrawal, so he gives him pills to take the edge off.

9:07 P.M. Jack grabs Claudia and tells her his real mission. He promises to save her and her family if she helps him. She agrees and they kiss.

9:10 P.M. Chase is beaten by Salazar's men, but he refuses to talk.

9:11 P.M. Claudia attempts to steal Hector's cell phone for Jack, but her plan fails.

9:18 P.M. Wayne briefs Palmer on CTU losing Jack. Campaign contributor Alan Milliken asks to see Palmer without Wayne.

9:22 P.M. Amador, the Salazars and Jack all meet. Amador reveals there is another buyer so there will be an auction for the virus. The other buyer arrives — Nina Myers.

9:30 P.M. Milliken tells Palmer that Wayne has been sleeping with his wife. Palmer refuses to fire Wayne despite Milliken's wishes.

9:36 P.M. Claudia dismisses Chase's torturer and she reveals Jack's plan to Chase.

9:37 P.M. The Salazars debate their bid and Jack reveals his history with Nina to them.

9:44 P.M. Michelle confronts Tony about his mistakes. She tells Chappelle that Tony needs to step down.

9:47 P.M. Palmer returns and confronts Wayne about the affair. He offers to resign.

9:48 P.M. Chappelle grills Tony on his competence and after some tests proves he is fit for duty.

9:55 P.M. Nina outbids the Salazars for the virus.

9:58 P.M. The Salazars pull over to kill Jack, but he convinces them to let him follow Nina and make the deal right. They agree.

Jack and Claudia make an agreement.

Nina Myers returns.

Wayne confesses his affair.

Nina Myers returned like a bad penny to torture Jack Bauer in season three, this time as a hired gun working for the highest bidder. A *24* veteran, Sarah Clarke says by the third season it was time to shake up the look of Nina Myers. "In season three, I really wanted something dramatically different to show the passage of time," the actress explains. "We went through some discussion about my hair. At first, we thought it might have some dramatic weird blonde streak. I was almost thinking it could be gray from the stress. We tried these two big blonde streaks on either side of my temples. I remember Kiefer walked into the trailer and said, 'Oh, *Josie and the*

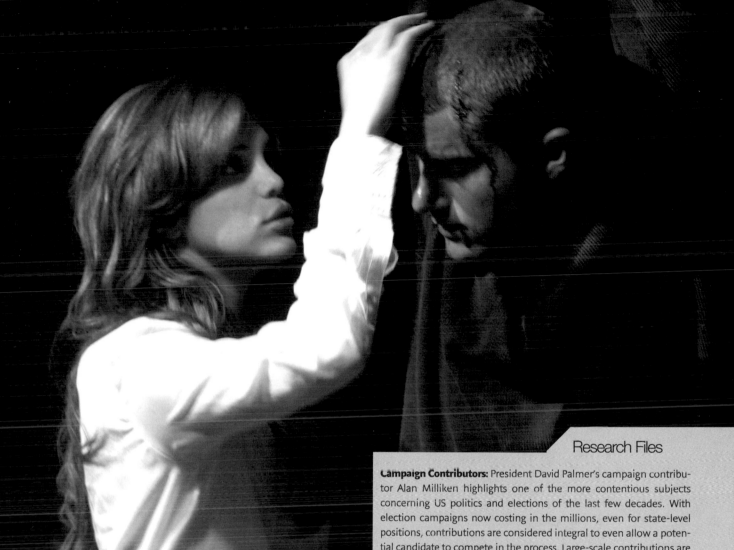

Pussycats.' It looked a little punk," she laughs. "My hair was still pretty short, it was chin length and it just felt too similar still. When we came up with the idea of the extensions, I was thrilled. I was hoping the producers would okay it, because it is time-consuming and costly. I was really excited that they agreed and went with it. Of course, once I did it — it was such a pain! I literally had two hundred little weaves and you have to get them tightened every month. It was so much pain to sleep on them! I slept on my face! But as much pain as it was, I am so appreciative of Susan Kelber, the hair stylist, and her dealing with the complexity of it. I felt it said so much, in the first moment of seeing her again, about the more mature nature of Nina without the government restrictions on her."

Research Files

Campaign Contributors: President David Palmer's campaign contributor Alan Milliken highlights one of the more contentious subjects concerning US politics and elections of the last few decades. With election campaigns now costing in the millions, even for state-level positions, contributions are considered integral to even allow a potential candidate to compete in the process. Large-scale contributions are often provided by corporations, lobbyists, unions and special interest groups that frequently expect legislation, funding or favors in exchange for their support. In recent years, the abuse of the system has caused Washington DC to enact legislation, like the 2002 Campaign Reform Act, in an attempt to try and keep the system as pure as possible. Results have been mixed, with partisan organizations being created to find ways to continue to increase revenue streams to their parties by creating work around organizations that bypass the current caps set for individual and corporate contributions.

Additional Intel

Sarah Clarke says she got to make personal selections for Nina's new look this season. "I got to pick a jacket from a designer I know that makes fabulous coats. My friend is a jewelry designer and she designed a necklace for me."

10:00 pm - 11:00 pm

Director: Brad Turner
Writer: Joel Surnow & Michael Loceff

Guest Cast: Gina Torres (Julia Milliken), Greg Ellis (Michael Amador), Sarah Clarke (Nina Myers), Penny Johnson Jerald (Sherry Palmer)

"What are you up to, Jack?" Nina Myers

Timeframe   Key Events

10:01 P.M. Hector calls Gael telling him they lost the virus to Nina and want it back. Jack is put on the line and CTU is able to trace his location.

10:05 P.M. Tony alerts Kim that Jack and Chase are alive.

10:07 P.M. Back at the farmhouse, Jack instructs Claudia to help save Chase.

10:11 P.M. Chloe gets an urgent call from Sarah who wants to meet her.

10:12 P.M. Hector shoots Chase in the hand.

10:17 P.M. Wayne briefs Palmer that three Senators dropped support of their health care bill due to Milliken.

10:19 P.M. Sarah is a teenager who drops her baby off with Chloe.

10:20 P.M. Gael provides Hector with Amador's location. Jack persuades the brothers to let him get the virus from Nina.

10:21 P.M. Claudia prepares her father and brother to escape.

10:28 P.M. Wayne meets with Milliken's wife in a bar. He wants her help in stopping Milliken. She refuses.

10:31 P.M. Claudia and Chase overcome Eduardo and kill him, Chase cauterizes his wound.

10:33 P.M. Chase, Claudia and her family race away with Hector shooting at them. Claudia is shot in the head.

10:40 P.M. Chappelle finds Chloe hiding the baby in CTU.

10:41 P.M. Jack and the Salazars arrive at the church where Nina is meeting Amador.

10:42 P.M. Jack is able to overcome Nina and he leads her into the church by gunpoint. She attacks him with her briefcase.

10:51 P.M. Chase calls Tony to brief him on Jack.

10:53 P.M. Jack tries to convince Nina to sell to the Salazars and that he is not working for CTU. She shoots her guard and asks Jack for the truth.

10:56 P.M. Wayne tells Palmer they will have to play dirty to fight Milliken. Palmer calls his ex-wife, Sherry.

10:59 P.M. Nina asks for forgiveness in killing Teri. Jack and Nina kiss.

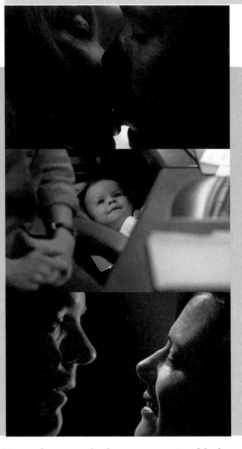

Wayne tangles with Julia again.

Chloe hides the mystery baby.

Nina toys with Jack.

Every time Nina Myers shows up, it always means trouble for Jack Bauer. In season three, Nina and Jack reunite with a shocking kiss. Sarah Clarke remembers, "The third season presented some interesting quandaries at first because they wanted to go for the ultimate shock. I still stand by the fact that if you have good characters, that is really what people are following. The adrenaline of the show is fantastic but if you over shock people they become a little numb. The original concept for the scene in the church when we got together was much more extreme. Let's put it this way, it wasn't just going to be a kiss," she laughs. "They wanted us to really be going at it, having sex, and I

just put up my hand and said, 'Look guys, we have to think of the reality here. Yes, I am a superpower and I can get out of a lot of things, but that situation puts me in a position of vulnerability, when I know these drug guys could be coming back and I know what Jack is capable of. So it doesn't make me powerful, it makes her weaker.' They just wanted it to be explosive but when we discussed it, we decided the kiss was all it needed to be.

"I also really appreciated that Kiefer allowed weakness in his character, which added to mine," Clarke continues. "He was really generous that way. In the church, it was his idea that he has a gun on me and he turns away and the minute he does, I whack him with the suitcase. It was all him and I was like, 'Thank you.' It shows that we are both highly thinking animals again that really have to watch each other every second. I am just as scared of him as he is of me and I don't feel confident that I can get away from him and neither does he."

Cauterizing: When Salazar shoots Chase's hand, he has to cauterize the wound to prevent continued bleeding and imminent infection. Cauterization is a medical term that means burning the body to close it. Known in the English language since 1541, cauterizing was originally a process where a piece of metal was heated over a fire and then applied to a wound to cause coagulation of the blood, stemming blood flow, but in turn causing extreme tissue damage. Nowadays, there are two forms of cauterization that are still in use with modern medicine: electrocautery and chemical cautery. Electrocauterization uses electricity instead of heat and is often used in breast mastectomy surgery. Chemical cautery is often used in dermatology with the removal of warts or other skin lesions.

Additional Intel

When Nina's passport is shown, there is on it an image of the actress and the alias name 'Sarah Berkeley'. That is, in fact, Sarah Clarke's real name, as she married fellow cast member Xander Berkeley (George Mason) in 2002.

11:00 pm - 12:00 am

Director: Jon Cassar
Writer: Joel Surnow & Michael Loceff

Guest Cast: Glenn Morshower (Agent Aaron Pierce), Mary Lynn Rajskub (Chloe O'Brian), Sarah Clarke (Nina Myers), Penny Johnson Jerald (Sherry Palmer)

> "Can you be a shark again Sherry?"
> President David Palmer

Timeframe

11:00 P.M. Adam locates Amador.

11:01 P.M. A Delta chopper picks up Chase and Claudia's family.

11:04 P.M. Palmer catches Wayne on the phone with Milliken. No one is willing to give in and Palmer says Sherry is needed.

11:07 P.M. Nina can tell Jack is lying. He overcomes her and admits he needs the deal to go through and she will get paid.

11:11 P.M. Hector calls Gael, who lies and says CTU has no idea where Chase is. Jack brings Salazar to Nina.

11:17 P.M. Sherry meets Palmer. She vows to help him.

11:20 P.M. Jack says Nina will help them. Salazar informs him of Chase and Claudia's escape.

11:22 P.M. Sherry admits she has dirt on Milliken she can use.

11:24 P.M. Chase is ordered to pull back because of Jack but he wants to track Amador.

11:25 P.M. Amador opens a case with the virus in a cylinder.

11:30 P.M. Wayne meets Sherry and asks her not to work against Milliken so Palmer will accept his resignation.

11:35 P.M. Nina whispers to Salazar that Jack is working for CTU. Amador calls and will complete the exchange.

11:43 P.M. Milliken tells the Palmers to have Sherry back down. Wayne calls the Mexican President about their virus operation.

11:46 P.M. The Salazars bicker about sticking to the deal. Jack secretly calls CTU but has to hang up when Ramon requests his phone back.

11:55 P.M. Chloe's crying baby disrupts CTU and Chappelle orders Kim to watch it.

11:56 P.M. Chase suits up with the commandos ready to raid the exchange.

11:57 P.M. The Salazars fight intensely about the safety of the deal. Ramon shoots Hector in the back to Jack and Nina's dismay.

Key Events

Hector discovers Claudia.

Sherry Palmer returns.

Ramon shoots Hector in the back.

The shooting of Hector Salazar by his brother Ramon was a turning point in the season. While tension had been mounting between the two men, audiences didn't expect the chilling outcome. Joaquim de Almeida reveals that the actual reason for the killing was a source of much debate. "We changed the last scene where I kill Hector. The reason I was supposed to kill him is that I find out his wife [Claudia] was having an affair with Jack. I expressed my concern to Kiefer — why would I kill my brother for that reason? He said, 'There is no way we can do this because it's getting too soap opera-ish.' I remember the day we were going to shoot the scene and the writers still hadn't

changed it. We started shooting and then we called the writers. We improvised what we thought the motives should be. We did the script rewriting and we ended up doing a whole different ending. I think the end that came out was much better. Now, I kill Hector because of the power struggle between two brothers and it made more sense. We thought the power struggle was what it was really all about. I remember being at a SAG [Screen Actor's Guild] panel, where they talked to me about playing such a bad guy, and that they felt for me because I shed a tear after killing my brother. I said, 'Bad guys are human and that's what happens to human beings. Even if the emotions can't be seen, they still have emotions, some more than others, but we still have to play them as bad guys.' I wanted to show the vulnerability of the character because otherwise, it's no fun. Characters that aren't vulnerable are no fun to play."

Research Files

Swiss Bank Accounts: The money being used for the virus auction is referenced in association with Swiss bank accounts. These types of accounts are known in international financial sectors for being the most secure and private accounts in the world. Swiss banks are the most discreet banking institutions, maintaining the utmost secrecy when it comes to satisfying a large portion of their client base's desire for anonymity. According to Swiss law, neither the bank's officers nor the bank's employees are allowed to reveal any information relative to an account to anyone, including the Swiss government. Of course, that kind of access and protection isn't cheap, as Swiss banks charge thirty five percent tax on interest earned in Swiss accounts, with Americans getting a thirty percent refund only when they reveal their identity and show proof they are not Swiss residents.

Additional Intel

Set decorator Cloudia Rebar works with production designer Joseph Hodges to create and dress all of the sets for each episode. Depending on what the script calls for, there can be as many as thirty sets per show. As a classical Feng Shui expert, Rebar infuses each set with the ancient Asian principles of balance and harmony.

Director: Jon Cassar
Story: Evan Katz & Stephen Kronish
Teleplay: Robert Cochran & Howard Gordon

Guest Cast: Vincent Laresca (Hector Salazar), Sarah Clarke (Nina Myers), Joaquim de Almeida (Ramon Salazar), Gina Torres (Julia Milliken)

"It was blood money, and I took it." Kevin Kelly

Timeframe	Key Events

12:02 A.M. Ramon berates Hector for not listening and kills him.

12:04 A.M. Sherry alerts Palmer she is meeting someone about Milliken.

12:06 A.M. Tony briefs CTU on the exchange. Chase is their connection to Jack on site.

12:09 A.M. Chase is able to overcome Salazar's guard, which thwarts Nina. Salazar threatens to kill Nina if she doesn't meet Amador.

12:16 A.M. Kim confronts Chloe about the baby and she says it is her boyfriend's. They are trying to protect the baby from her abusive mother.

12:18 A.M. Sherry meets with Kevin Kelly, who was paid off by Milliken when he killed Kevin's daughter in a car accident. Sherry offers Kevin a better deal.

12:22 A.M. Tony orders the Delta team in for the virus exchange.

12:28 A.M. Sherry calls Palmer with the plan for Kevin's pardon in exchange for his testimony on Milliken.

12:30 A.M. Kim tells Tony she believes Chloe is unstable and the baby story is untrue. Tony says he needs Chloe for this mission now.

12:33 A.M. Amador arrives and speaks with Nina, who demands to verify the virus.

12:40 A.M. Wayne calls Tony, livid at the secret plan. He demands a briefing.

12:43 A.M. The exchange happens.

12:44 A.M. Nina gives Salazar the briefcase. Salazar pulls a gun on Jack.

12:45 A.M. Chase shoots Salazar in the shoulder. Nina runs into the woods. Jack pursues Salazar and the virus on foot.

12:51 A.M. Sherry calls Milliken's wife with a plan.

12:54 A.M. Chase and Jack find an injured Salazar with the vial. Jack begs him to give it up. The vial explodes.

12:56 A.M. Jack calls Tony and says the virus was switched by Amador. Chloe tracks Amador's location. The Delta team is ambushed by Amador's men and he escapes.

12:59 A.M. Amador reveals the real virus in his pocket.

The exchange happens...

The Delta team observes...

All hell breaks loose!

One of the weaker sub-plots of the season was the introduction of a baby into CTU by Chloe. Hidden under Chloe's desk as a favor to someone outside the office, the baby became an odd sore thumb amidst the virus crisis. While it was later revealed to be Chase's baby, the actors all admit trying to sell the storyline was tough going at times. James Badge Dale admits he loved the season, but wasn't very fond of the baby storyline. "The Kim stuff was good because it gave us something to focus on and play with when working with Kiefer or Elisha. We didn't delve into it very much, but it helped the audience relate to Chase a little more and brought us all closer

together in a more coherent storyline. As far as the baby stuff, I never really understood it. Ninety-nine percent of us were like, 'Why? Why? Why? Why do we need this baby?' It never went anywhere. Cute baby though," he laughs.

Fellow actor Paul Schulze, who played Ryan Chappelle, concurs, adding, "The baby was very difficult. The producers are smart and if the show was only about anthrax on the back of a van and whether it was going to be released or not, it would be tense but become one note and hard to live with. So these guys mix in all kinds of things." Schulze admits he got the idea that Chloe was in a pinch. "Given the rigors of her schedule, she has no alternative but to bring it into CTU. But for me to literally march up some stairs and threaten to fire somebody and be completely undone by the whines of an infant was challenging, but we made it work. There were some of us that were like, 'My God, what are we doing?' But it's always a challenge to make a show no matter what the show is about and for actors to be completely committed to and honest about whatever situation they are asked to be in, so that one was a challenge and it was fun to rise to it."

Research Files

Spectroscope: Spectroscopes are used in astronomy and chemistry for spectroscopic analysis of materials. Basically, when certain materials are heated, such as sodium, they emit light that is characteristic of the atomic makeup of the material. Different elements make different colors when they glow and the spectroscope spreads out the colors of the light, making it easier to identify the elements by the bright lines seen in the spectroscope. In modern cell studies, spectroscopes are utilized to separate information about species, structures, and molecular conformations within the cell.

Additional Intel

Before becoming widely known for *24*, Mary Lynn Rajskub was best known for her stand-up comedy and sketch comedy work on shows like *Mr Show with Bob and Dave*, *The Larry Sanders Show* and *Late Friday*.

David Palmer

Experience:

President of the United States
United States Congress – Senator (MD)
Senate Appropriations Committee – Member
Senate Commerce Subcommittee – Member
United States Congress – Representative (MD)
House Ethics Committee – Chairman
House Ways and Means Committee – Member
House National Security Subcommittee – Member
Maryland State Congress – Representative (Baltimore)
Fidley, Barrow & Bain – Attorney at Law

Education:

University of Maryland School of Law – Juris Doctorate
Georgetown University – Bachelor of Arts, Political Economy

Honors:

NCAA All-American – Men's Basketball
Big East Conference – Defensive Player of the Year
Sporting News – College Player of the Year
Wooden Award for Player of the Year

Personal:

Divorced
Son – Keith Palmer
Daughter – Nicole Palmer

Sherry Palmer

Experience:

Congressional Spouses Club – President
USO World Board – Appointee
Congressional Wives for Human Rights – Fundraising Chairwoman
Maryland Hunger Fund – Chairman of the Board

Education:

Georgetown University – Bachelor of Arts, Sociology

Personal:

Divorced
Son – Keith Palmer
Daughter – Nicole Palmer

1:00 am - 2:00 am

Director: Bryan Spicer
Story: Robert Cochran & Stephen Kronish
Teleplay: Joel Surnow & Michael Loceff

Guest Cast: Paul Schulze (Ryan Chappelle), Mary Lynn Rajskub (Chloe O'Brian), Penny Johnson Jerald (Sherry Palmer), Sarah Clarke (Nina Myers)

"Nina… I know what you've done, and how you've managed to stay alive is impressive. But if you try and play Jack one more time, he's gonna kill you."
Chase Edmunds

Timeframe

1:00 A.M. Jack and Chase look for Nina. She overcomes Chase but Jack cold cocks her. She says she can help them get Amador in LA.
1:08 A.M. Sherry calls Palmer and says she is approaching Milliken's wife.
1:10 A.M. Jack, Nina and Chase take a Navy plane to LA.
1:11 A.M. Amador calls Marcus Alvers about the virus.
1:19 A.M. Jack gets Nina to reveal Amador's connection – Alvers. Tony runs a check.
1:20 A.M. Chase and Jack have a heated discussion about trust.
1:21 A.M. A CTU tech finds an Anthrax connection between Alvers and Amador.
1:22 A.M. Nina admits she knows more about Alvers and demands Jack's help with the Dept. of Justice in exchange. He agrees. She provides him an Internet socket to contact Alvers.
1:24 A.M. CTU's network shuts down. Nina has uploaded a worm.
1:29 A.M. Jack tells Tony to put Chloe on the worm.
1:30 A.M. Nina demands they return to Mexico and she will slow the worm down, protecting CTU agents from exposure.
1:31 A.M. Chappelle allows Chloe to work on the worm.
1:33 A.M. Sherry meets Milliken's wife at their home, poses her plan and requests Milliken's cell phone.
1:42 A.M. Sherry gets the phone, but Milliken enters. Sherry threatens him about Kevin's payoff.
1:44 A.M. Jack forces Nina to help Chloe slow down the worm.
1:46 A.M. Sherry and Milliken fight. He has a heart attack and dies.
1:52 A.M. Sherry convinces Milliken's wife to cover up what happened.
1:56 A.M. Chloe cracks the worm and the plane lands in LA.
1:59 A.M. Chappelle gets Chloe to admit the baby is Chase's and Kim finds out.

Key Events

Nina unleashes a worm in CTU.

Milliken dies of a heart attack.

Chloe saves the day.

Reflecting back on season three, actor Kiefer Sutherland says one of the most compelling aspects of the year was his partnership with Chase Edmunds. Usually a loner on the job, Edmunds was the first official partner Jack was paired with on the series. Sutherland says that relationship brought new facets of Jack's personality into play. "I think the dynamic that I thought was interesting, from my perspective as an actor, was working with [James] Badge [Dale], who played Chase. I love working with him. He is a great actor and I thought he did an amazing, amazing job. The dynamic onscreen was of these two guys who were responsible for each other's lives and all of a sudden to cross over into this very

personal world with my daughter, on some levels, is a real violation of this trust that is between these two partners in law enforcement. It was something we got to play on through the whole year and it was a real counterbalance between this feeling of broken trust and this absolute respect for each other which partners have. It was an interesting dichotomy to play. I think the dynamic was really effective and I enjoyed our scenes a lot."

Sutherland also loved getting to play against Sarah Clarke's Nina Myers for one last round. "In a blog I once read, someone had written a list: 'If Jack Bauer Could...' and one of them was, 'If Jack Bauer was in a room with Hitler, Stalin, and Nina Meyers, and he had a gun with 2 bullets, he'd shoot Nina twice.' I always thought that was a very funny perspective on just the amazing amount of hatred there is in him for her. It was so deeply personal. She took his wife, they had had an intimate relationship too, and she put his daughter through amazing risk. As much as she and I as actors wanted to play out this thing that we had started, I believe that people wanted to see her end."

Research Files

Worm: When Jack connects to the socket, Nina is able to get him to download a worm into the CTU server. A computer worm is one of the most destructive programs hackers have developed to cause considerable damage to technology and businesses around the globe. Worms are self-replicating computer programs that harm networks and the flow of information. A paper published in 1982 about the new threat coined the term from *The Shockwave Rider*, a science fiction novel published in 1975 by John Brunner. One of the first worms of note was the Morris worm created by Robert Tappan Morris in 1988. It infected huge numbers of computers and caused disruptions with networks. Morris was found and convicted under the US Computer Crime and Abuse Act. Currently, popular modes of distributing worms are through email, instant messaging, file sharing and IRC chat channels. Anti-virus and anti-spyware software are successful ways to protect computers from worms.

Additional Intel

Day three begins three years after the events of season two, placing the timeline of the show around September 2008. The show never provides an actual year for any season, but producers confirm that the show takes place in the not too distant future.

Director: Bryan Spicer
Writers: Howard Gordon & Evan Katz

Guest Cast: Penny Johnson Jerald (Sherry Palmer), Lothaire Bluteau (Marcus Alvers), Sarah Clarke (Nina Myers), Gina Torres (Julia Milliken)

> "You don't have any more useful information, do you Nina?" Jack Bauer

Timeframe

Key Events

2:00 A.M. Jack and Nina deplane. Chase gets a call from Chloe about the baby.

2:04 A.M. Wayne debriefs Palmer that the virus is in LA. Sherry calls and says she never went to Milliken's.

2:08 A.M. Jack and Kim reunite at CTU. Kim is shaken to see Nina.

2:13 A.M. Jack admits to Kim he will need rehab. Kim sees Chase and looks away.

2:18 A.M. Tony is assigned the interrogation of Nina. Michelle is concerned because of their past together.

2:19 A.M. Tony grills Nina about Alvers and reveals he has HIV. Nina's pulse spikes.

2:21 A.M. Amador and Alvers exchange the virus in a seedy bar.

2:27 A.M. Chase comes clean to Kim about his baby.

2:29 A.M. Chappelle forces Jack to speak to an investigator about his heroin addiction.

2:32 A.M. Tony sends for the torture specialist for Nina.

2:38 A.M. The investigator questions Jack about the timeline of his drug use. Chappelle wants to adjust the truth and Jack refuses.

2:41 A.M. Palmer assembles his Cabinet to develop a covert and public containment strategy for the virus.

2:42 A.M. Wayne briefs Palmer on Milliken's death. Palmer confronts Sherry and she eventually admits she was at his house but she did nothing to him.

2:48 A.M. The specialist inserts a needle into Nina's neck too deeply.

2:54 A.M. Palmer tells Wayne Sherry's version of the story. Wayne calls Milliken's wife and gets the truth.

2:55 A.M. Nina is rushed out of CTU, unshackled, and she is able to pretend to pass out.

2:56 A.M. Jack runs to the clinic and Nina is gone. Chappelle locks down CTU.

2:57 A.M. Kim runs into Nina and threatens to shoot her. They have a standoff. Nina is shot in the shoulder as Jack comes from behind Kim. Nina pleads for her life. Jack shoots her three times.

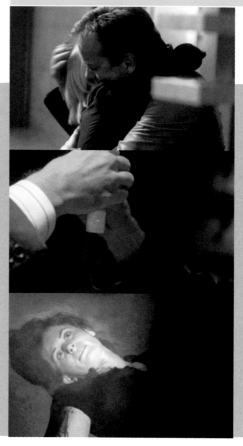

Jack and Kim bond once again.

Amador and Alvers exchange the virus.

Nina Myers is dead.

All good villains on *24* eventually have to die and season three was the third strike for Nina Myers. Sarah Clarke says she was very pleased with her arc and that she didn't overstay her welcome. "I know on this show, particularly, to be a man is very powerful. So the fact that they sort of made me like a man means I got to do a lot of great things. Of course, I was exhausted by the end of it. As much fun as it is to play a villain, when you are bringing a modicum of reality to it, it can be quite draining, so it was the perfect amount of time." Reflecting on her final scenes, Clarke smiles, "The ultimate powerful thing would be if Nina was like, 'You will not get

anything from me,' but then I love that I go into surgery and kill everyone but the woman."

As it often happens on the series, the final confrontation between Jack, Kim and Nina was initially very different. Elisha Cuthbert reveals, "In the script, I was originally supposed to kill her, but Kiefer came on set that morning and said, 'I want to kill her.' I remember actually arguing that I thought I should kill her. He had killed so many people already and there was a lot of meaning behind it for me. Nina had killed my mother on the show and now I was an agent and old enough and it was my way of saying, 'I deserve to be here.' Somehow he stole it from me, but I guess you can't say anything to Jack," she laughs. Clarke admits she is happy Jack was the one who did her in. "I think I would have been really horrified if Kim killed me. As much as I love Elisha Cuthbert, she is a wonderful actress, just integrity wise, but Nina is the much stronger woman. At that point she did feel like a caged animal and it made the most sense that it was Jack killing her. I was sad of course — they did talk about me getting away, but Kiefer was like, 'Come on! I am the worst Federal Agent there is if I let her get away again!'"

Research Files

Angina: When Sherry and Julia Milliken surprise Alan Milliken, it sets off his angina. Angina is intense chest pain due to a lack of oxygen supply attributed to coronary artery disease. An angina attack, such as Milliken's, can come and go, but any spasms lasting more than fifteen minutes often signify a heart attack. Attacks are often triggered by exertion or emotional stress and can be alleviated by rest or specific angina medication. Risk factors for angina include cigarette smoking, high cholesterol, diabetes and high blood pressure. About 6.3 million Americans experience angina and, surprisingly, women are more prone to attacks than men.

Additional Intel

According to costume designer Jim Lapidus, for every main character on the show, the costume department has to buy or create six to twelve versions of every piece of costume in order to accommodate not only the main actor, but their photo doubles and stunt doubles.

3:00 a.m - 4:00 a.m

Director: Kevin Hooks
Story: Michael Loceff
Teleplay: Robert Cochran & Howard Gordon

Guest Cast: Paul Blackthorne (Stephen Saunders), Greg Ellis (Michael Amador), Lothaire Bluteau (Marcus Alvers), DB Woodside (Wayne Palmer)

"I just want this day to end." Michelle Dessler

Timeframe   Key Events

3:01 A.M. Chappelle angrily confronts Jack about Nina. Jack says it was self-defense.

3:04 A.M. Amador provides the virus to a man named Saunders, who says he wants to send a message.

3:05 A.M. Tony briefs CTU on Nina and widening the search for Amador and Alvers.

3:06 A.M. Saunders demonstrates a detonating device to Amador and Alvers and belittles them for their shoddy and greedy work.

3:09 A.M. Chappelle's interrogation of Jack is interrupted by a lead on Amador. Chappelle reluctantly lets Jack back in the field.

3:15 A.M. Milliken's wife calls Wayne for help. Wayne lies to Palmer that he has spoken to her.

3:19 A.M. Wayne confronts Sherry about the Milliken cover-up and she convinces him to help her keep the truth buried.

3:21 A.M. A detective talks to Milliken's wife and starts to believe someone else was at the house.

3:23 A.M. Adam tracks Amador's active bank account and Jack and Chase hit the road.

3:30 A.M. The detective calls Sherry and confronts her with Milliken's wife's story. She denies it all and says the President will confirm her alibi.

3:33 A.M. Jack and Chase raid the club and subdue Amador.

3:40 A.M. Jack confronts Amador but he won't reveal the virus' location. Jack has Chase slice Amador's palm.

3:42 A.M. Jack briefs CTU. Amador's laptop has schematics for the Chandler Hotel.

3:45 A.M. Chappelle assigns Michelle as the best person from CTU to handle the hotel.

3:53 A.M. Gael identifies Alvers in the hotel. NHS has not arrived so Michelle and Gael go in ahead against protocol.

3:55 A.M. Alvers sets up the virus detonation device in the ventilation room.

3:56 A.M. Michelle comes upon Alvers and handcuffs him to a pipe. He admits he released the virus.

3:58 A.M. Gael finds the detonator, it explodes in his face, releasing the virus into the building.

Saunders sends a message.

The Chandler Hotel is the target.

The virus detonates.

One of the few familiar faces to make it out alive season after season was Secret Service Agent Aaron Pierce. Assigned to David Palmer from season one, Agent Pierce became a steady presence for both the President and the audience over the years. A stalwart counsel and protector to the office, actor Glenn Morshower says the role surprisingly evolved over the seasons. "My initial take on it was that Pierce was extremely peripheral, at best, a third tier character who was just there to serve the President and nothing more," the actor says of his role. "The deeper we got into it, it became apparent there was chemistry between Palmer and Aaron as

friends, as someone Palmer trusted. Then they just built on that and the whole thing has snowballed. I know that they are as surprised by the way the character has unfolded as I am. I was originally hired for two episodes. What happened was that Dennis [Haysbert] and I really liked each other as people and the more they saw that, the more they wrote for Palmer and Pierce. We are actually good friends which made it work on every level. There was no pretending that we adore each other. We are brothers. He was with me when my dad died. We've just supported one another through a number of different events."

Research Files

Detonator: The virus is rigged to a detonator that explodes in Gael's face. Detonators are devices used to trigger explosives and can be as simple or complicated as the user needs them to be. The most common kinds are mechanical or electrical, with chemical detonators being a less common option. The primary explosive for many mechanical detonators is an ASA compound, which is comprised of lead azide, lead styphnate and aluminium. Another popular explosive that releases less lead in the air — for environmental protection — is DDNP (diazo dinitro phenol). There are three kinds of electrical detonators: instantaneous electrical detonators (IED), short period delay detonators (SPD) and long period delay detonators (LPD). None of them utilize an explosive; rather a shock wave is created by vaporizing a length of thin wire by an electric discharge. These options are accurate to the nanosecond.

Additional Intel

Actor Glenn Morshower's real name is Glenn Bennett. The native Texan took the name of his stepfather and used it as his professional name throughout his career.

4:00 am - 5:00 am

Director: Kevin Hooks

Writers: Evan Katz & Stephen Kronish

Guest Cast: Andrea Thompson (Nicole Duncan), Mary Lynn Rajskub (Chloe O'Brian), Paul Blackthorne (Stephen Saunders), Penny Johnson Jerald (Sherry Palmer)

"We found the incubator with the virus in it in the room next door. If you don't tell me what I need to know, I'll put you in there, and I'll open it up." Jack Bauer

Timeframe

4:00 A.M. Alvers tells Michelle there are eleven more vials of the virus, but he doesn't know where. Tony orders her to leave the building, but she refuses.

4:05 A.M. Jack can't get any more info from Amador.

4:08 A.M. Chappelle orders the hotel under quarantine.

4:09 A.M. Michelle shuts down the hotel and blocks cell phones to suppress a panic.

4:11 A.M. Amador escapes. Kim calls Jack and alerts him. Jack and Chase follow him.

4:16 A.M. Palmer tells Wayne to alert the Governor of the hotel outbreak. Sherry tells Palmer Milliken's wife confessed. She demands he corroborate her 'alibi'.

4:20 A.M. Amador calls Saunders and tries to lose Jack and Chase.

4:22 A.M. Tony asks Duncan about Michelle's potential fatality rate. She doesn't know.

4:23 A.M. The hotel is infected and Gael shows symptoms.

4:29 A.M. Michelle presses Alvers to reveal how they altered the virus.

4:30 A.M. Wayne pressures Palmer to lie for Sherry. Palmer refuses.

4:31 A.M. Michelle calls Tony and says Alvers added an accelerant to the virus. Tony is upset.

4:35 A.M. A panicked bellhop pulls the fire alarm to escape but Michelle is able to convince them it is a false alarm.

4:41 A.M. Kim is able to track Amador and give Jack his location.

4:50 A.M. Palmer corroborates Sherry's story to the detective. Palmer tells Sherry he despises her.

4:54 A.M. Jack and Chase watch Amador open a briefcase and it explodes. Saunders calls Jack and threatens to open the other eleven vials unless Jack helps him contact someone.

4:56 A.M. The hotel is in a panic and Michelle has to shoot a guest to get the riot to stop.

4:58 A.M. Jack connects Saunders with the President.

Key Events

Gael shows symptoms.

Palmer lets Sherry have it.

Michelle takes charge.

The addition to the Palmer family in season three was Wayne Palmer, David's brother and White House Chief of Staff. Serving dual roles in his brother's life, Wayne revealed his own checkered past throughout the season, including some poor decisions and moral quandaries, which in turn end up affecting Palmer's political destiny. Season three afforded actor DB Woodside some very juicy moments to play. The actor offers, "One was when Wayne jumped on the bandwagon with his sister-in-law, Sherry [Palmer]. Wayne comes into the President's office late at night to give him some normal news, and then he tries to persuade his brother that he needs to lie to

the Chief of Police so that blame doesn't fall back on him because of Sherry's actions. In that scene they have their first, I think, in that season, big confrontation. What I loved about it was that there you have these two noble, in a sense, African American men in the two most important positions in our country and yet they are brothers. So they have a very professional relationship, but because Wayne is both his brother and the White House Chief of Staff, at any time, as long as it was behind a closed door, he could drop the veil of being Chief of Staff and be his brother and be his family. He could get a lot more personal with him than probably most people would, or should. During that scene, I think you see the moment when the veil drops and they are just two brothers arguing."

Research Files

Quarantine: When Alvers releases the virus into the ventilation system of the Chandler Hotel, the entire building is forced into a lockdown quarantine to try to contain the spread of the deadly toxin. The word quarantine literally comes from the Medieval French phrase *une quarantaine de jours*, which means a period of forty days. The first documented case of quarantine dates back to 1377 when the city of Dubrovnik kept passengers of arriving ships isolated to help prevent the spread of the Black Death. The practice was extremely effective in stopping the plague and throughout the centuries has been an effective tool to contain disease from rampant spread. One of the most recent global quarantine events occurred in 2003 with the SARS virus. Today in the United States, the Division of Global Migration and Quarantine, part of the CDC's National Center for Infectious Diseases, takes care of all domestic quarantines.

Additional Intel

DB Woodside is also a musician and a director. He directed his first short film in 2006, co-starring himself and former *24* alum Reiko Aylesworth.

5:00 am - 6:00 am

Director: Ian Toynton
Writers: Robert Cochran & Stephen Kronish

Guest Cast: Paul Blackthorne (Stephen Saunders), Jesse Borrego (Gael Ortega), Paul Schulze (Ryan Chappelle), Andrea Thompson (Nicole Duncan)

> "No, you don't negotiate with terrorists. Well, I don't negotiate with heads of state, so just do what you're told."
> Stephen Saunders

Timeframe   Key Events

5:00 A.M. Michelle tells the hotel patrons the truth and has to fire her gun once more to get them in line.

5:04 A.M. Palmer tells Wayne they must give in to Saunders' demands to save lives.

5:05 A.M. Michelle calls Tony, upset she had to kill someone.

5:07 A.M. Duncan arrives at the hotel. Michelle forces Alvers to ID his boss. Chloe cross checks Jack's file and sends headshots to Michelle's laptop. Eventually, Alvers identifies Stephen Saunders, a British agent who worked on the Victor Drazen case.

5:15 A.M. Palmer, Wayne and Homeland Security Chief Joseph O'Laughlin discuss how to prepare but not alert the press.

5:17 A.M. Saunders calls Palmer and demands the Secret Service pick up a package in ten minutes.

5:19 A.M. Jack theorizes about Saunders with Chase. Jack calls an MI-6 friend who finds a woman, Diana White, who may be the connection to Saunders.

5:21 A.M. Agent Pierce brings Palmer the package – an untraceable cell phone. Saunders demands Palmer call a press conference and say, "the sky is falling". He agrees.

5:28 A.M. Chase finds out Diana White is a high paid escort with a rich client list.

5:29 A.M. Tony desperately calls NHS for possible cures. Chappelle tells him to refocus and exact revenge for Michelle through his work.

5:32 A.M. Jack and Chase find Diana's home. She threatens to shoot but they grab her and take her to MI-6.

5:44 A.M. Palmer says the phrase at the press conference.

5:45 A.M. At MI-6 they are attacked by a helicopter and Diana is killed.

5:46 A.M. Jack and Chase manage to retrieve the hard drive with Saunders' file.

5:58 A.M. Saunders calls Palmer and orders Chappelle to be killed or he will unleash the virus.

Agent Pierce explains the package.

Palmer holds the press conference.

A helicopter attacks Jack and Chase.

As the hotel virus lockdown story progressed, the character of Michelle Dessler had to stand up to the panicking hotel guests. In a surprisingly hard line stance Michelle shoots a guest intent on escaping out the window of the lobby. She has to keep the virus from spreading, so she shoots him dead. Actress Reiko Aylesworth says the hotel arc was Michelle's defining storyline. "In the story I created for her it was the first time she took a life. She had no choice because he would hurt other people. So dealing with that event and having that blood on her hands... It's funny because some of the heaviest acting in those scenes was done on a cell phone. The whole Tony and Michelle relationship

really came into its own that way. It was so intense and I'm glad I got a chance to work on it."

In regards to her relationship with Tony during season three, the actress continues, "Torture has been a big thing on *24*. Also, putting your relationship aside and sacrificing the person you love. Jack has had to do that too. In that sense, what they are dealing with is: how much do you give up before you lose your humanity? With Jack especially, you see him being torn down so much, and you wonder at what point does he cross over into being no better than what he is chasing down? It's the same with our country. It draws real parallels. We say in times of crisis, we are going to lay down the law. Okay, but how much do you do that before what you are protecting has been defiled so much that it's not what it was anymore. *24* is great because it really reflects on both the political and the personal realm."

Research Files

MI-6: The Secret Intelligence Service (known as MI-6) is the UK's external security agency that handles all covert operations over seas. Captain Sir George Mansfield Smith-Cumming was the first director of the branch and he went by the code name 'C'. Adopting a single letter became the standard over the years for directors and became the model for spy novelist Ian Fleming's directors in his James Bond books (ie 'M'). Since 1995, MI-6 headquarters have been located in an impressive building at 85 Vauxhall Cross, along the river Thames. In September 2000, the Real IRA attacked the structure with a Russian-built Mark 22 anti-tank missile, but no structural damage was incurred. Interestingly enough, the actual MI-6 headquarters was used as a location for a James Bond film for the first time ever in 1991 for *The World is Not Enough*. Prior to that movie, Her Majesty's government objected, citing security as the issue.

Additional Intel

During the many cell phone conversations between Michelle and Tony at the hotel, Reiko Aylesworth and Carlos Bernard made sure they were there for one another in reality, as both actors read their lines off camera to the other so they could achieve the right emotion and reality for the scenes.

6:00 am - 7:00 am

Director: Ian Toynton
Writers: Howard Gordon & Evan Katz

Guest Cast: Paul Schulze (Ryan Chappelle), Christina Chang (Dr Sunny Macer), Paul Blackthorne (Stephen Saunders), Daniel Dae Kim (Agent Tom Baker)

"Sorry we let you down, Ryan. God forgive me."
Jack Bauer

Timeframe / Key Events

6:02 A.M. Jack returns to CTU with the hard drive. Chappelle debriefs him on the money trail to Saunders. The President calls Jack.

6:03 A.M. Palmer explains Saunders' demand.

6:05 A.M. Jack orders Chloe to switch the Saunders search back to CTU.

6:06 A.M. Michelle breaks down to Tony when he has suicide pills delivered to her.

6:07 A.M. Jack tells Tony about the possible Chappelle-Saunders connection.

6:09 A.M. Jack reveals Saunders' demand to Chappelle, who is confused too. Jacks asks Chappelle to give his files to Chloe.

6:17 A.M. Michelle tells the infected they will die in six hours. She offers them suicide pills. A guest alerts Michelle that a man she had a one night stand with is missing from the hotel.

6:21 A.M. Jack orders Chloe to break the encryption faster and Kim offers to help. Chappelle goes missing.

6:22 A.M. By orders of the President, Chappelle is remanded to a holding room.

6:30 A.M. William Cole enters his house. His nose is bleeding.

6:31 A.M. Chloe and Kim decrypt the account and find a local address. CTU sets up a raid.

6:32 A.M. Jack escorts Chappelle to the helicopter in case they have to meet Saunders' deadline.

6:40 A.M. Chase and another agent arrive at the address where Saunders is traced.

6:42 A.M. Jack and Chappelle land at the train yard.

6:43 A.M. Chase finds the apartment empty.

6:47 A.M. Jack gets a call from Saunders to leave Chappelle's body in a van.

6:52 A.M. Macer arrives at the hotel with suicide pills. The woman photo IDs the missing man.

6:56 A.M. Jack walks a shaking Chappelle to the yard. He makes him kneel. Chappelle begs to take his own life, but he can't pull the trigger. Jack shoots him in the head.

Michelle breaks down to Tony.

William Cole shows symptoms.

Jack kills Chappelle.

Cast, crew and critics often cite this episode as one of the most gut-wrenching hours of *24* ever because of Jack's sanctioned killing of Ryan Chappelle. For as brutal as the end sequence is, director of photography Rodney Charters says it was even worse before network changes. "Fox got cold feet over how powerfully we told the story and they made us back away because it was way too scary and violent. We had in fact played the whole shot in long shot, from the point of the view of the van drivers, including the bullet and the blast from the head and the falling forward. It was too much, it was the kind of thing you would be shocked to see in a feature."

Paul Schulze, who played Chappelle, says he's proud that his character's death had such an impact on audiences. "If I had to go, and I *had* to go, I was really grateful that they decided to create something as dramatic as it was. The episode was one of the few times that the action, from the decision to the killing, all happens in one episode. It's like a movie. Most serial television would have definitely milked it for several episodes." As to whether he and Kiefer made any changes to the final scene, the actor says. "No, it stayed close to script. By the end, what was finally shown, there were a few things that were cut, but it was close. When we rehearsed it that day, I was completely filled with emotion and everybody was anticipating a fairly smooth and fun shoot. But when we started to shoot, it became increasingly difficult for me to really engage emotionally. I think there might have been a part of me that was like, 'If I don't give them what they want, they might not kill me.' Kiefer could see I was struggling a little bit and was there to help me. Eventually, it became easier for me to relax and let some emotions out."

Research Files

Incubation Period: Gael and Michelle wait inside the hotel under quarantine to determine the incubation period of the virus, from initial exposure to the first signs of symptoms. The official medical term is the 'latency period' and depending on the pathogen it can take from minutes to years. The incubation period is the time when a person may carry the disease and may or may not be able to spread it to someone else. All diseases have different latency periods but some of the more recognizable gestation periods include: cholera (1-3 days), influenza (1-4 days), measles (9-12 days), chicken pox (14-16 days), and mumps (14-18 days). For the majority of diseases, adults have the longest latency period, while children or infants have the shortest latency periods. The virus on *24* was engineered to be more potent and become lethal in a matter of hours.

Additional Intel

This episode is one of the rare *24* episodes not to end with the traditional ticking clock sound. Chappelle's death is honored with the silent clock. Paul Schulze says the cast and crew presented him with a black funeral wreath for his death that he then put in his house.

Tony Almeida

CTU Missions:

Operation Proteus, 2000 (Special Commendation)

Experience:

CTU – Special Agent in Charge, Los Angeles Domestic Unit
CTU – Deputy Director, Los Angeles Domestic Unit
Transmeta Corporation – Systems Validation Analyst

Expertise:

Certified Instructor, Krav Maga hand-to-hand combat
defense

Education:

Stanford University – Masters of Science, Computer
Science
San Diego State University – Combined Bachelor of
Engineering/Bachelor of Computer Science

Military:

US Marines – First Lieutenant
Scout-Sniper School (3rd Marine Division)
Surveillance & Target Acquisition Platoon School (1st
Marine Division)

Personal:

Married – Michelle Dessler (CTU employee)

Michelle Dessler

Experience:

CTU – Intelligence Agent, Los Angeles Domestic Unit

CTU – Internet Protocol Manager, Los Angeles Domestic Unit

DARPA – High Confidence Systems Working Group

National Institute of Standards & Technology – Computer Security Division

Expertise:

Built IPSec architecture

Attacks scripts, computer vulnerabilities, intrusion detection, penetration testing, operational security, viruses

Proficiency in Cerberus and PlutoPlus

Education:

University of California (Davis) – Bachelor of Science, Computer Science

Personal:

Married – Tony Almeida (CTU employee)

7:00 am - 8:00 am

Director: Jon Cassar
Writer: Michael Loceff

Guest Cast: Paul Blackthorne (Stephen Saunders), Paul Schulze (Ryan Chappelle), Alan Dale (Vice President Jim Prescott), Maria del Mar (Rachel Forrester)

"Saunders is going to know we have his daughter."
Kim Bauer

Timeframe	Key Events

7:00 A.M. Men with the van arrive and take Chappelle's body.

7:03 A.M. Jack calls Palmer, who refuses any more of Saunders' demands. He convenes his Cabinet.

7:05 A.M. Chloe, Kim and Adam discover Saunders has a daughter in Santa Barbara. Jack suggests they plant a look-alike agent so they can pick up his real daughter without him realizing.

7:08 A.M. Chase heads to the infected Cole's house.

7:09 A.M. Kim ends up being the closest match to Saunders' daughter. Kim agrees to the mission.

7:17 A.M. Chase reveals Cole's actions to his wife and sees the bloody tissue.

7:18 A.M. Cole infects people at a pharmacy.

7:19 A.M. Jack returns to CTU and Tony tells him Kim is going on the case.

7:20 A.M. Jack and Kim argue over the mission.

7:26 A.M. Jack escorts Kim to the helicopter, gives her a gun and they both get inside.

7:27 A.M. Palmer briefs his Cabinet on the virus.

7:30 A.M. Chase is angry to hear Kim is in the field.

7:32 A.M. Cole enters the hospital and is quarantined.

7:37 A.M. Saunders gets Chappelle's body and makes sure his daughter is under surveillance.

7:30 A.M. Saunders calls Palmer and demands a list of all foreign nationals working covertly as spies in one hour.

7:42 A.M. Techs prep Kim to look like Saunders' daughter.

7:49 A.M. Agents find Saunders' daughter and spill a drink on her so she goes to the bathroom. Inside, they drug her and Kim switches clothes to take her place.

7:51 A.M. After talking to Cole, Tony determines that more than 75 people might be infected and two entire neighborhoods.

7:53 A.M. Jack talks to Saunders' daughter and she refuses to help him.

7:57 A.M. One of Saunders' men grabs Kim at gunpoint.

7:58 A.M. Kim struggles with the man and shoots him, blowing their cover to Saunders.

Cole infects the pharmacy.

Jane Saunders talks to Jack.

Kim Bauer saves herself.

In the last half of the season, Stephen Saunders (Paul Blackthorne) took over from the Salazars as the main villain being pursued through to the finale. Executive producer Howard Gordon says the character was actually born out of negative feedback from the previous year. "One of the big criticisms of season two was that our villain, Peter Kingsley, was too cardboardy. It had nothing to do with actor Tobin Bell. He did a great job. But we always try to retrofit the next year based on what we learned, and the idea was to have a villain who really was a formidable point-of-view character and we got that with Saunders."

One of the strengths of *24* is the caliber of talent that is attracted to the show, especially those who make the villains come alive. Kiefer Sutherland offers, "We have been really fortunate, and I can say this really about all the actors that have worked on *24*, people who come on for just a day or two all the way to cast members. We have been so lucky and fortunate to have the quality of actors that we've had, always. It's one of the main reasons why the show has done as well as it has, because there is no part that is too small. People have come in and done amazing stuff really quickly. We've had tons of great, great actors. All of the villains we've had have been very responsible in filling out their requirements. In that I mean if you break the idea of acting down to being in a band... Not everybody can be the lead singer, not everybody can be the lead guitarist. You need the drummer, the bass player and you need the horn section, and really good actors take pride in playing all of those different 'instruments'. The actors we have had look where they are supposed to fit and then they do that, and we've been really lucky to have that. It's not always the case, I can assure you," he laughs.

Research Files

Santa Barbara: Stephen Saunders' daughter lives in Santa Barbara, a city eighty-five miles northwest of Los Angeles. Known as the 'American Riviera', due to its temperate weather and affluent citizens, Santa Barbara is located on the Pacific coast. The city also fosters a very lively artistic and education community with the UC Santa Barbara campus operating within the city limits. With its roots in Spanish heritage, the city maintains a unique appearance due to its Spanish Colonial architectural style, with many buildings featuring the trademark red tiled roofs. The city does not allow billboards in town or on the freeway, maintaining a crisp, unobstructed view to the ocean for residents and tourists alike. Famous people who were born in Santa Barbara include football player Randall Cunningham and model Kathy Ireland.

Additional Intel

Saunders provides President Palmer with a website: www.sylvia-imports.com. The website is real and owned by *24* director of photography Rodney Charters. The message on his site says: "A Big Thank-you from the crew of *24*. Thanks for watching, we love making it for you, and yes, we did get picked up for Season 4."

8:00 am - 9:00 am

Director: Jon Cassar
Writer: Virgil Williams

Guest Cast: Paul Blackthorne (Stephen Saunders), Christina Chang (Dr Sunny Macer), DB Woodside (Wayne Palmer), Alexandra Lydon (Jane Saunders)

> "Chloe, I'm getting really tired of your personality!"
> Tony Almeida

Timeframe / Key Events

Jack calls for Saunders.

Tony calls for a 'Code 9'.

Saunders escapes.

8:00 A.M. Two more infected people are identified and containment becomes the goal.

8:04 A.M. Jack talks to Saunders' daughter. He briefs her on her father's history and provides evidence of the terrible things he is now responsible for. She gives Jack her father's emergency number.

8:09 A.M. Macer tells Michelle her lab results are in.

8:14 A.M. Agent Pierce tells Palmer it's not safe for him to stay in the state, but Palmer fights to stay.

8:17 A.M. Palmer refuses to cave to Saunders' demands, so Jack uses his daughter as a hostage. He asks her to call him so they can trace his location.

8:19 A.M. Palmer misses the deadline, so Saunders calls to release the virus in San Francisco. His cell rings and it's his daughter. He knows she is with Jack.

8:21 A.M. Adam and Chloe trace the call. Chase and Jack go to Saunders.

8:27 A.M. Michelle calls to tell Tony she is immune to the virus.

8:30 A.M. Palmer talks to the press about the best way to handle the virus.

8:33 A.M. Saunders knows CTU has located him but he chooses to wait. One of his henchmen balks, so he shoots him. He calls another one of his men and asks about a mystery woman.

8:34 A.M. Kim takes Saunders' daughter back to Los Angeles.

8:41 A.M. Adam's sister is diagnosed with the virus.

8:45 A.M. Agents surround Saunders' building and Jack calls up to Saunders with a bullhorn telling him they have his daughter.

8:54 A.M. Saunders manages to get men to kidnap Michelle as she is leaving the hotel. He contacts Tony and demands that he send the agents into the front of his building or he will take Michelle's eyes out. Tony agrees.

8:58 A.M. Tony calls the agents and Saunders escapes out the back unnoticed.

The virus storyline was one that hit Reiko Aylesworth particularly hard due to the parallels to what was going on in real life in the US after 9/11. A resident of New York City, Aylesworth says, "I remember being in New York with all the anthrax fears. It was scary. So to look out to fifty extras [on the hotel set] and see them look back at you crying... It was some of the best acting I had seen. I was looking at background actors who were *so* engaged. We were all working these late nights so we were tired and broken down. They gave me the most realistic looks when I had to make the speech about who was testing positive for this virus. I was looking out and seeing children who had

Police Codes: Law enforcement have long used codes for transmissions between dispatch and the location of an incident to speed up the request for additional services or to provide specifics to assess the situation for future action. A popular code system, called ten-codes, has long been used by law enforcement to represent common phrases in voice communication. The codes, including ten-four for 'message received' and ten-zero for 'use caution', were originally created to make a simple, concise system to speed up communication in times of crisis. Over the years the code system has become so varied and complicated due to changes on local, regional and national levels, that ten codes is being phased out for more clear, specific language. Response codes are another form of shorthand that developed in North America and primarily refer to emergency response actions, for example Code One — no lights and sirens; Code Two — lights only, no siren; and Code Three — lights and siren.

Additional Intel

Production designer Joseph Hodges re-created the CTU logo after the pilot and it has been used to this day. The reworked logo is based on his love of Formula One cars, specifically using colors that are inspired by the high performance cars.

a day to live and were going to die a horrible death, and it's not complete fiction. It was so intense with this feeling like you were responsible," she shudders.

This episode features one of Aylesworth's favorite moments of the season: when she calls Tony and lets him know that she is immune to the virus. Praising the work of director Jon Cassar in particular, the actress remembers, "You see my relief. I'm fine. I tell him I'm fine and I hang up and then the camera pans to the officer right next to me who gets bad news. That is what makes the scene because it's all about survivor's guilt too."

9:00 am - 10:00 am

Director: Frederick K. Keller
Writers: Joel Surnow & Michael Loceff

Guest Cast: Alexandra Lydon (Jane Saunders), Zachary Quinto (Adam Kaufman), Geoff Pierson (John Keeler), Jamie McShane (Gerry Whitehorn)

"The only thing that matters is stopping Stephen Saunders." President David Palmer

Timeframe

9:00 A.M. Jack orders the building to be gassed. He questions Tony's decision for SWAT formation and Chase finds Saunders has escaped.

9:05 A.M. Saunders calls Tony and threatens to kill Michelle unless his daughter is released.

9:06 A.M. Palmer calls Tony and finds out Saunders is gone.

9:09 A.M. Kim and Saunders' daughter arrive at CTU.

9:15 A.M. Chloe realizes satellite images of Saunders' building have been deleted. She surmises a mole is helping him inside CTU.

9:19 A.M. Tony and Saunders agree to let one another talk to their hostages.

9:21 A.M. Chloe gets a call from Macer looking for Michelle.

9:22 A.M. Adam tells Tony there has been a breach in security and Tony locks down CTU. He lies and tells Chloe that Michelle is somewhere safe.

9:28 A.M. Sherry calls Senator Keeler and wants to meet him.

9:31 A.M. Jack confronts Tony about a mole in CTU and catches him in a lie.

9:32 A.M. Sherry offers to confess to her part in Milliken's death so Palmer will drop out of the race when blackmailed about the truth. In return, she wants a position on Keeler's staff.

9:41 A.M. Wayne tells Palmer that Sherry went to talk to Keeler.

9:44 A.M. Jack confronts Tony about his lies and he confesses. Jack takes Tony out of command.

9:47 A.M. Tony calls Saunders in a panic and Saunders demands his daughter is taken out of the building.

9:55 A.M. Chloe identifies Tony as the mole from a voice recording. Tony locks her in the tech room.

9:56 A.M. Tony grabs Saunders' daughter.

9:59 A.M. Tony drives to meet Saunders, meanwhile, Jack locks down CTU. Keeler requests a meeting with Palmer.

Key Events

Sherry meets with Keeler.

Tony traps Chloe.

Jane Saunders is taken by Tony.

09:57:44

At the end of the season, Tony Almeida is faced with a huge moral quandary — save the life of his wife or stop Saunders and the virus. The scenario set up one of Carlos Bernard's favorite scenes on the show. When Jack discovers Tony's duplicitous actions in CTU, it gets ugly. "I really love the scenes towards the end of the third season where Tony and Jack were going at each other over the whole Michelle thing," the actor reveals. "I give Saunders the information he needs and I am going to get Michelle. I love those scenes with Jack and I know Kiefer feels the same way. When our characters come up against each other, it is a lot of fun. Tony is the audience's way

in. Jack is a little hard to relate to because he is such a machine when it comes to crossing that line. Tony makes a lot of mistakes because of his emotions, and because he is not like Jack. When the two characters get together, it is an interesting contrast. Some of the best scenes are when Jack and Tony butt heads and go at it with each other. Ultimately, they are shooting for the same goal; they just think differently."

Does Bernard agree with Tony's decision of personal life before country? "No, I don't think he did make the right decision, but that is the thing I like about the character — he is flawed. He would like to believe he is built for that job, and I don't know that he is. His emotions get in the way. That is the thing I like about the show. It is constantly asking, 'What would you do if you were put in that position?' The truth is you can sit back as an audience member and say, 'Well, that was just a wrong move. Why would he do that?' But until you are put in that position, I don't think each individual knows what he would do."

Research Files

Lockdown: Tony orders a lockdown of CTU after Adam alerts him to a breach in the system. An official lockdown is an emergency protocol used to prevent information or people from escaping an area. It's meant as an official means of controlling a problem before key people or data are lost or disseminated. Lockdowns are often instituted during a time of crisis such as the aftermath of the 2005 London Underground attacks, where London was locked down to prevent further attacks and enable law enforcement to track suspects with tighter constraints. Lockdowns are also common in prisons, when acts of violence erupt that can quickly turn into riots. These need to be contained immediately to prevent death or injuries to both inmates and guards. On *24*, CTU has been locked down on many occasions since the first season.

Additional Intel

Video computer playback operator Dan Murbarger reveals that all the TV news footage that runs on the screens in CTU is shot specifically for the show, using real anchors from Los Angeles Fox affiliates to create pieces that his department is responsible for playing back.

10:00 am - 11:00 am

Director: Frederick K. Keller
Story: Robert Cochran & Howard Gordon
Teleplay: Evan Katz & Stephen Kronish

Guest Cast: Penny Johnson Jerald (Sherry Palmer), Paul Blackthorne (Stephen Saunders), DB Woodside (Wayne Palmer), Geoff Pierson (John Keeler)

"I want to stay with you, and I would raise a child with you, Chase. I just won't raise one for you." Kim Bauer

Timeframe — Key Events

10:00 A.M. Jack goes to find Tony.

10:05 A.M. From her cell, Michelle taunts her captor about his imminent death when the virus is released.

10:06 A.M. Kim and Chase talk and she says she will stay with him if he transfers out of field work.

10:09 A.M. Jack catches up to Tony and says he knows he is trying to save Michelle. Jack says he needs Saunders' daughter now. Tony provides the phone booth location to call Saunders.

10:17 A.M. Keeler meets Palmer and accuses him of covering up the Milliken death and shows Sherry's proof. He demands Palmer steps down after the crisis.

10:20 A.M. Tony goes to the phone with Jack's orders to reject the initial location.

10:22 A.M. Saunders refuses a change and Jack hangs up. Tony is angry and they fight. Saunders calls again with a new location.

10:28 A.M. Chase sets up his team under the Sixth Street Bridge.

10:30 A.M. Palmer calls Sherry and she admits what she did and that Keeler offered her respect. She says she will go to jail to make Palmer pay.

10:34 A.M. Michelle pretends to have symptoms so she can trick her guard and knocks him out. She takes his gun and cell.

10:35 A.M. Michelle is blocked and can't get through to CTU on the cell.

10:41 A.M. Wayne proposes stealing the evidence.

10:44 A.M. Michelle contacts Jack. He asks her to get recaptured to force an exchange. She agrees.

10:52 A.M. The meeting takes place on the bridge.

10:55 A.M. Saunders shows himself and both sides start firing. Saunders escapes in a helicopter. Jack calls for air support.

10:57 A.M. F/A-18 jets fire on the helicopter and it explodes.

10:59 A.M. Jack finds Saunders in the wreckage and demands the other virus vials.

Saunders runs to escape...

F/A-18s fly overhead...

Jack finds Saunders.

One of the biggest visual stunts the show ever pulled off was the flight of two F/A-18 jets overhead for the climatic scene when Saunders' helicopter is shot down. Location manager KC Warnke says the whole sequence happened relatively easily considering the seemingly impossible logistics. "The F-18 was interesting because no one had ever done it. I think that it started out for us because we shot out at Point Magoo when we needed a naval base. We started talking to the military and the guy at the Pentagon who was in charge of the base was a huge fan of the show, so we developed relationships with the military through that connection. It all started with a production meeting where someone went, 'We

should fly an F-18 overhead,' and then everyone went, 'Yeah, right!' Next thing you know you make a call and two months later it happens. Since then we have worked with the military maybe six or seven times."

Going over the production specifics, fellow location manager John Johnstone details, "The F-18 was one of the most thrilling shots because it presented the greatest challenge in terms of coordination. You first start out asking the question — who should we talk to first? The military. That led to the next person we needed to talk to at the FAA [Federal Aviation Administration] and the response from that person when we said where we were from was, 'Oh, that's my favorite show!'" he laughs. "It was actually fun creating the scenario and the military coming back to us and saying they could work with it. They came back to us with our plan basically in their format. They treated it almost like an air show, with the whole logistics planned down to the second. That conversation led to another conversation including the City Council, the City Permit Office, LA Fire Department, the *LA Times*, a couple of radio stations and a couple of TV stations, culminating in a paper notification for almost a two mile radius. We got people to pass out flyers door-to-door and office-to-office. We were confident that we tried to get to as many people as possible. Out of all of that we only had one complaint."

Research Files

F/A-18 Hornet: When Saunders attempts to escape by helicopter, President Palmer calls out the big guns with two F/A-18s sent into Los Angeles airspace to stop him. The 'hornet' is an attack fighter for both ground and aerial targets. The jet was originally designed in the seventies and is currently used by both the US Navy and US Marine Corps. The F/A-18 is a twin engine, mid-wing, multi-mission tactical aircraft. The jet is known for its superior maneuverability, high angle-of-attack handling and easy maintenance for less downtime. Outside the US, the jet is also used by air forces in Canada, Australia, Spain, Kuwait, Finland, Switzerland, and Malaysia.

Additional Intel

In 2006, *24: The Game* was released for Sony's PlayStation 2. The videogame takes place between seasons two and three of the series and answers vital questions about Jack and Chase's first meeting and how Palmer survived the flesh-eating virus.

11:00 am - 12:00 pm

Director: Jon Cassar
Story: Evan Katz & Stephen Kronish
Teleplay: Robert Cochran & Howard Gordon

Guest Cast: Penny Johnson Jerald (Sherry Palmer), Paul Blackthorne (Stephen Saunders), DB Woodside (Wayne Palmer), Mark Rolston (Bruce Foxton), Randle Mell (Brad Hammond)

"When your daughter is infected, I'm gonna make you watch her die." Jack Bauer

Timeframe   Key Events

11:00 A.M. Saunders says the other vials will be released at noon. He will provide the locations if Palmer lets him escape to North Africa.

11:09 A.M. Palmer and Wayne set Sherry up to keep her distracted while Wayne looks for the evidence.

11:10 A.M. Jack takes Saunders to the hotel and threatens to put his daughter inside unless they get the other vials. Saunders relents.

11:18 A.M. CTU finds ten of the eleven vials. Arthur Rabens has the last vial in Los Angeles and Saunders doesn't know where he is releasing it.

11:19 A.M. Jack asks Tony's replacement, Brad Hammond, to go easy on Tony. Hammond doesn't care.

11:21 A.M. Tony returns to CTU in cuffs.

11:23 A.M. Milliken's wife calls Wayne and says she is being arrested for murder. She asks for his help, but he hangs up when Sherry drives away. He then breaks into Sherry's house.

11:31 A.M. Sherry meets Palmer and he offers her a job. She says she wants to be First Lady again and he agrees. Sherry is suspicious and says she will side with Keeler.

11:36 A.M. Palmer calls Wayne with a warning.

11:37 A.M. Chloe confirms Rabens is in LA.

11:42 A.M. Michelle finds out what Tony did to protect her.

11:43 A.M. Jack and Chase track Rabens to the Metro system.

11:44 A.M. Sherry returns home to find Wayne. The agent tackles her and finds the evidence taped to her back.

11:53 A.M. Agents try to find Rabens without knowing what he looks like. Jack realizes Rabens slipped the transmitter onto someone else.

11:57 A.M. Milliken's wife arrives at Sherry's house and threatens to shoot her. Sherry promises to get her a pardon, but Milliken's wife fires twice and kills her. She then turns the gun on herself.

11:59 A.M. Jack and Chase start searching the trains for Rabens.

Tony returns in handcuffs.

Sherry meets her end.

Julia takes her own life.

Executive producer/creator Robert Cochran says it was clear to the creative team that Sherry Palmer's story came to its appropriate conclusion with her death. "When a situation presents itself where a death works dramatically, we almost always do it. Sherry Palmer is the flipside of David Palmer. She is the dark side of politics. She is Lady Macbeth. You can do that story and find different angles on it, like using the Palmer's divorce, so there were things to play, but eventually you feel like you've played it out. To go to that well one more time on our show – on a pure soap opera, that's what the show is and it's expected, but on our show, it's not. If we had to find another way

for Sherry to be manipulative or devious we would have been, as writers, bored with it, and we always feel like the audience is going to be tired of it pretty quickly too. I also think if you keep bringing the same people back, doing the same thing, you verge on campiness if you're not careful."

Sherry being involved in David's political life again allowed the writers to give the President a darker side. "Palmer was a noble character and a great President and that's the way we played him for two seasons. But from a dramatic point of view, that gets boring after a while," Cochran says. "Not that nobility is a boring thing, but play it week after week, and we were asking, without losing his essential character, what could we do? We didn't want to turn him into a bad guy, so we ended up having him make all these choices, where there is *no* good choice. In the end, he had made so many of these decisions that he, himself, came to the conclusion that he could no longer carry on in this position, which in a sense protected his nobility and his sense of the office, while not backing off on the hard choices he had to make. We felt it was a good balance for him and people still loved the character and nobody felt he was sullied by what happened."

Research Files

Los Angeles Subway: Arthur Rabens is tracked down to the Los Angeles Metro Rail underground. The busiest of the four Metro Rail lines in Los Angeles, the Metro Red Line averages over 138,000 daily weekday commuter boardings. The Red Line is primarily underground, as opposed to the other light rail lines, and has expanded over the years, first opening in 1993, with the final section of the line in Hollywood being opened in 2000. The Red Line uses seventy-five-foot electric multiple unit cars, usually using six cars at a time during peak times. Trains running to Wilshire/Western have a maximum of four cars. The Red Line has been featured many times in TV and film. Most recently in *Alias* which used the Civic Center station as its secret headquarters. The movies *Volcano*, *S.W.A.T.*, *Speed* and *The Italian Job* all featured large action sequences involving the Metro.

Additional Intel

According to actress Reiko Aylesworth, she and Carlos Bernard found out about a year after they were working together that they were both born in Evanston Hospital in Chicago, Illinois, ten years apart.

12:00 pm - 1:00 pm

Director: Jon Cassar
Writers: Joel Surnow & Michael Loceff

Guest Cast: Kamala Lopez Dawson (Theresa Ortega), Michael Cavanaugh (Homeland Security Director Joseph O'Laughlin), Salvator Xuereb (Arthur Rabens), DB Woodside (Wayne Palmer)

"There's some things I have to do, but I'm going to be fine." Jack Bauer

Timeframe	Key Events

12:00 P.M. Michelle tries to have Saunders ID Rabens.

12:05 P.M. Gael's wife arrives at CTU. She sees a picture of Saunders.

12:17 P.M. Chloe calls Kim to leave Gael's wife and help her transport Saunders.

12:09 P.M. As Saunders looks at the monitor, Gael's wife walks up and shoots him dead.

12:15 P.M. Wayne returns to Palmer and debriefs him on Sherry. Palmer is upset by Wayne's callousness and calls his children about their mother.

12:19 P.M. Chase shares with Jack that after this mission he is transferring out of the field to be with Kim and his child.

12:21 P.M. A detained passenger runs. It's Rabens, who pulls a car jacking to escape. Jack and Chase follow.

12:28 P.M. Michelle asks Hammond to allow Tony to assist in the chase for Rabens. He agrees.

12:30 P.M. CTU cars block Rabens, who escapes into a school. Jack calls for a lockdown.

12:39 P.M. In a science lab, Rabens attacks Chase. They fight and Chase clamps the virus device to his arm. Rabens activates the device. Jack comes in and kills him.

12:41 P.M. Jack has four minutes to dismantle the device, but he is unable to do it. Chase tells Jack to leave, but he refuses.

12:45 P.M. Chase tells Jack to use an ax on the wall to cut his arm off. Jack does and races with the device to the teacher's lounge where he throws it in a sealed refrigerator. It detonates, but is contained.

12:51 P.M. Tony is put back in custody and he kisses Michelle goodbye.

12:53 P.M. Palmer calls Jack to apologize about Chappelle and to reveal he won't be seeking re-election.

12:56 P.M. Kim sees her father and tells him Chase will recover.

12:58 P.M. In his SUV, Jack privately breaks down in tears until CTU summons him back to the job.

Jack chops Chase's arm off.

Palmer talks to Jack.

Jack breaks down.

Finale episodes are always full of resolution, a huge one this season being the virus. Chase Edmunds loses his arm to stop it. Actor James Badge Dale remembers, "They gave me a rubber hand and there was one point where my hand was tucked into my sleeve, and Kiefer had this rubber axe. He's staring at me with that look on his face and I'm like 'Oh man. Don't hit me!' And he's going 'I'll try not to.' We were both a little nervous. They did this wide shot where Kiefer comes down, cuts off the hand, picks it up, moves it over, takes the virus thing, I pass out, and he runs out the room. They call 'Action!' Kiefer cuts the hand off, he nicks the rubber hand, the hand literally flies twenty

feet across the room but he didn't see it go. You just see it shoot across the room and he's standing there and can't find the hand. He's looking all over for it and finally just turns and goes 'Where the f*** is the hand?'"

For actor DB Woodside the hardest moment to play of the series was when David Palmer decided not to run a second term. "As a character, it was *extremely* hard because here was someone who Wayne believed that this country needed. For David not to run again because of Sherry, as Wayne would put it, this small obstacle in the road of life, he just can't get past that. As a character, I think it was a crushing defeat. As the actor, I was sad because I was thinking, 'How are they going to bring him back?' he laughs. "I think it's very difficult to lead with the kind of integrity that Dennis's character had in that office nowadays. I think we want someone who we may not necessarily want to have over for dinner, but they are protecting us. So it was a great moment. It was the culmination of those three years of being such an amazing human being, while at the same time running for the highest elected office in the country."

Research Files

Amputation: Jack has to separate Chase from the virus detonator by chopping off his arm. Amputation of appendages has been around as long as humans have existed. Usually, amputation is a form of surgery used in extreme situations to control pain or stop the spread of infection that leads to gangrene. In some Islamic countries, amputation of hands or feet is considered an accepted punishment for criminals, while other communities consider finger or toe amputation the completion of a ritual to adulthood.
The reattachment of amputated limbs, replantation, is a fairly new microsurgical process that is extremely lengthy and difficult to accomplish successfully. The process entails reconnecting blood vessels, muscles, tendons, nerves, and other soft tissues, and aligning or fixating bony structures. Afterwards, the rehabilitation process to get partial to normal use of the limb takes months if not years, depending on the limb.

Additional Intel

24 won four Emmy Awards for season three: Outstanding Casting for a Drama Series, Outstanding Single-Camera Picture Editing for a Drama Series, Outstanding Single-Camera Sound Mixing for a Series, and Outstanding Stunt Coordination.

Regular Cast:
Kiefer Sutherland (Jack Bauer)
Kim Raver (Audrey Raines)
Alberta Watson (Erin Driscoll)
William Devane (Secretary of Defence James Heller)
Mary Lynn Rajskub (Chloe O'Brian)
Roger Cross (Curtis Manning)
Lana Parrilla (Sarah Gavin)

7:00 a.m. - 8:00 a.m.

Director: Jon Cassar

Writers: Joel Surnow and Michael Loceff

Guest Cast: Logan Marshall-Green (Richard Heller), Nestor Serrano (Navi Araz), Louis Lombardi (Edgar Stiles), Jonathan Ahdout (Behrooz Araz), Shohreh Aghdashloo (Dina Araz)

> "What we accomplish today will change the world. We are fortunate that our family has been chosen to do this."
> Navi Araz

Timeframe

7:00 A.M. Brody sits on a train with a briefcase cuffed to his wrist. The train hits a truck and explodes. A man pulls up to the wreckage, shoots an injured Brody and takes the briefcase.

7:03 A.M. Chloe O'Brian and Sarah Gavin at CTU get a lead on local Turkish terrorist Tomas Sherak.

7:04 A.M. CTU head Erin Driscoll gets word on the train bomb.

7:05 A.M. Jack Bauer and Audrey Raines get dressed in a hotel room. She asks if he is concerned about returning to CTU.

7:10 A.M. Sherak calls Navi Araz and tells him they have the briefcase. Navi tells his son Behrooz to take the briefcase from Sherak to a warehouse.

7:20 A.M. A programmer named Andrew finds destructive code from Turkey on the Internet.

7:22 A.M. Jack and Audrey meet her dad and their boss, Secretary of Defense James Heller.

7:23 A.M. Andrew calls his friend Chloe about the code. Chloe briefs Driscoll, who tells her to pass it to the FBI.

7:25 A.M. Jack walks into CTU and meets his replacement, Ronnie Lobell.

7:29 A.M. Jack talks to Driscoll about the CTU budget. She excuses herself to watch a raid on a Turkish laundry.

7:30 A.M. Jack watches the feed and because of his advice, they arrest Sherak.

7:39 A.M. Heller arrives at his son Richard's house.

7:44 A.M. Hit men attack Andrew's office but he escapes on a bike.

7:49 A.M. Jack finds out from Chloe there may be an 8:00 a.m. attack.

7:54 A.M. Jack calls Audrey urgently needing Heller's help for clearance.

7:57 A.M. Sneaking into Sherak's interrogation, Jack shoots him in the leg and determines Heller is a target.

7:58 A.M. On the phone with Audrey, Jack hears them get attacked and kidnapped.

7:59 A.M. Navi gets the briefcase.

Key Events

The train explodes.

Jack returns to CTU.

The terrorists come for Heller

As is customary for all the *24* season openers, co-executive producer and director Jon Cassar is responsible for getting the season off the ground with a literal bang. In season four, not only was there a massive train wreck in the opening minutes, but there was also the frighteningly realistic Heller kidnapping at the end of the hour. While these huge set pieces are a hallmark of the show, Cassar says they don't entirely define *24*. "First of all, we are always called an action show and nothing upsets me more than calling us an action show because all the imitators that have come out and have tried to do an anti-terrorist show, I think that's where they put all their money. After a year, they are off the air because people aren't interested. We really aren't an action show. We really are a character-based show wrapped around some of television's best and most realistic action. Saying that, I'm

proud we upped the ante on [the action] this year. In year three, we moved away from it a little bit and in year four, I wanted to pump up the action. We had a fantastic sequence right off the top when Heller and Audrey get kidnapped. We tried to move away from the typical Hollywood action, so it feels like you are watching the news. The way I designed the whole Heller kidnapping was that I didn't even tell the camera guys what was going to happen. It was orchestrated as one big theater piece. They walked out of the house, these trucks came out of nowhere and it was all done at once. The camera guys were just spinning. They were like, "Ok, pan over there! There's a car moving – pan over there!" If you watch that sequence, it really is raw and it feels so real and so scary because of the way we shot it."

Research Files

Secretary of Defense: James Heller is the Secretary of Defense for President John Keeler at the start of season four. The President appoints the actual position of Secretary of Defense (SoD) with approval by the Senate. Any candidate considered must be a civilian who has not served in the military for ten years. As the primary defense policy advisor to the President, the SoD formulates and executes defense initiatives for the nation. The Secretary oversees the Department of the Army, Department of the Air Force, Department of the Navy, along with other defense agencies and commands. Other responsibilities include being a member of the President's Cabinet and of the National Security Council. Within the military, the Secretary is known as SecDef. Together with the President, they make up the National Command Authority, the sole people allowed to launch strategic nuclear weapons.

Additional Intel

For the first time ever in the US, Fox decided to run the entire season of 24 without pre-emptions. Therefore, the fourth season premiered in January 2005 and ran repeat-free through May.

8:00 am - 9:00 am

Director: Jon Cassar
Writer: Howard Gordon

Guest Cast: Tony Plana (Omar), Louis Lombardi (Edgar Stiles), Logan Marshall-Green (Richard Heller)

> "Apology accepted. But if you try to exceed my authority again, I will stop you cold." Ronnie Lobell

Timeframe — Key Events

8:01 A.M. Heller and Audrey are bound and transferred to another van.

8:02 A.M. Driscoll has Jack arrested.

8:07 A.M. Chloe goes to Jack to alert him of the Turkish code.

8:08 A.M. A hit man, Kalil, kills Andrew's mother and taps into a call between Jack and Andrew.

8:11 A.M. Dina Araz offers to take the briefcase instead of her son. Navi refuses.

8:12 A.M. Jack confronts Driscoll. He demands to be reinstated. He is made an auxiliary agent under Lobell.

8:19 A.M. Heller and Audrey are put into an underground compound. Omar decides to hold Audrey for leverage.

8:23 A.M. Behrooz prepares to leave with the briefcase, but his girlfriend calls.

8:31 A.M. Ronnie and Jack leave to get Andrew. Ronnie threatens Jack.

8:33 A.M. Heller and Audrey are in a caged cell. Henchmen come in and force Heller out of his clothes.

8:35 A.M. Behrooz drops the briefcase off at Omar's compound. Debbie follows and confronts him in front of the henchman.

8:42 A.M. Agent Curtis Manning submits Richard to a lie detector test.

8:44 A.M. Navi slaps Behrooz when he returns home. Navi is livid and demands his son call Debbie to their house.

8:46 A.M. Jack and Lobell arrive to get Andrew, but Kalil poses as Jack and gets to him first.

8:53 A.M. An officer sees Kalil take Andrew to a car.

8:54 A.M. Kalil is stopped in traffic. Lobell wants to apprehend him. Jack argues that following him may lead to Heller. Lobell knocks Jack down and handcuffs him to a railing.

8:56 A.M. Lobell approaches the car and is shot. Kalil runs. Jack screams for the keys, which Lobell throws to him then dies. Jack goes after the terrorist.

8:58 A.M. Omar broadcasts streaming video to CTU of Heller and says he will be tried for war crimes.

Navi slaps Behrooz.

Jack calls to a shot Lobell.

Heller is a hostage.

The on-screen roller coaster ride of *24* is often just as dizzying for the actors bringing the drama to life. Actress Kim Raver was brought in to play Audrey Raines, Jack Bauer's lover and the daughter of Secretary of Defense James Heller, played by William Devane. Raver says she got off the plane and was immediately thrust into the insanity of production. "Literally, the train took off out of the station and it just picked up speed and was crazy. My first day with William, I was handcuffed, blindfolded and gagged and thrown into a van with him," she laughs. "You can imagine, we are rolling around in the back of this van as it screeches out of there. My butt is in his face and his butt is in my face and we're literally like, "Hi, nice to meet you!"" Despite the awkward first meeting, Raver says she loved working with Devane and they had an immediate familial chemistry. "We connected and found this father/

Research Files

Lie Detector Test: Richard Heller is required to take a lie detector test to prove his innocence of his father's kidnapping. Officially known as a polygraph, the test monitors several physical factors (like elevated blood pressure, heart rate and respiration) to determine whether a person is being truthful when questioned by an examiner. John A. Larson invented the polygraph and today there are two varieties: computerized and analog. While polygraphs have been determined to be very reliable, there is no scientific evidence or published studies that provide absolute numbers or statistics as to their validity. Experts also admit that the success of a test is greatly determined by the success of the queries provided by the examiner and how well the subject can lie and control their bodies throughout the test. In the US, no one can be forced to take a polygraph and according to the Supreme Court case *United States v. Scheffer* (1998), it's up to individual police jurisdictions as to whether the results can be submitted to court as evidence.

Additional Intel

Shortly after the premiere of season four, Fox released its first *24*-inspired mobisode called *24: Conspiracy*. It features new actors, but takes place around the Heller kidnapping.

daughter relationship pretty quickly. It's rare. Usually, you have to work on these relationships but everything was so fast and so furious. You just either have to step on board and go for the ride or you kind of get left behind." Raver credits the *24* creative team with making her transition so comfortable. "I definitely felt like I was in amazing hands and maybe that's where the trust comes from. With something of the caliber and quality of *24*, and to know that I was in Jon (Cassar's) hands and Kiefer's hands and Joel (Surnow's) hands, I just kind of dove off the cliff."

9:00 am - 10:00 am

Director: Brad Turner
Writer: Evan Katz

Guest Cast: Tony Plana (Omar), Aisha Tyler (Marianne Taylor), Myndy Crist (Melissa), Lukas Haas (Andrew Paige), Leighton Meester (Debbie Pendleton)

> "Forget about me. You have to take every chance. Promise me." *Secretary of Defense James Heller*

Timeframe   Key Events

9:00 A.M. President Keeler updates his Cabinet on Heller.
9:04 A.M. Jack calls Driscoll about Lobell's death. The line dies and Driscoll informs CTU that Jack is off the case.
9:07 A.M. Kalil calls Omar, who orders him to lose any pursuers. Jack enters on-coming traffic to keep up.
9:08 A.M. Omar demands Heller sign a list of offenses or they will kill Audrey. Heller relents.
9:15 A.M. Driscoll debriefs the President.
9:17 A.M. CTU tech Marianne Taylor calls Curtis accusing him of impacting her job because they once had an affair.
9:18 A.M. Jack calls Chloe asking for satellite tracking help. She agrees.
9:19 A.M. Driscoll brings Marianne on as a consultant. Curtis determines Richard may be withholding information.
9:21 A.M. Behrooz tells his mother about Navi's demands. She agrees to talk to her husband.
9:28 A.M. Curtis brings in a torturer for Richard. Curtis balks, which infuriates Driscoll. They compromise with Curtis' non-invasive technique.
9:30 A.M. Dina talks to Navi about Debbie.
9:31 A.M. Kalil pulls over and warns Andrew.
9:32 A.M. Jack sees Kalil's men beating Andrew.
9:34 A.M. Kalil gets Andrew to confess the code he saw then calls Omar.
9:35 A.M. Jack tells Chloe he will follow Kalil, then shoots the two men about to kill Andrew.
9:42 A.M. Heller tells Audrey she may be able to escape when the trial begins.
9:47 A.M. Chloe tinkers with fellow tech Edgar Stiles' computer to boost her satellite tracking signal for Jack.
9:49 A.M. Richard undergoes sensory disorientation, but he refuses to talk to Curtis.
. **9:55 A.M.** Marianne gets Edgar to fill her in on Jack and Driscoll. Jack sees Kalil at a convenience store.
9:57 A.M. Debbie arrives at Behrooz's for tea with Dina.
9:58 A.M. Jack dons a mask and pretends to hold up the store.

Richard gets tortured for the truth.

Dina unfurls her nasty plan.

Jack becomes a robber!

Season Four found *24* revisiting the use of Middle Eastern terrorists as the villains for the year. But rather than just re-treading familiar territory, the producers took the opportunity to give the story a more realistic spin. Co-executive producer and director Jon Cassar says making the bad guys three-dimensional has always been their goal. "It's always a challenge to make these evil bad terrorists real because they are real people that have their point of view. As mad as we might think it is sometimes, it is a point of view that is grounded in some kind of reality for them. As horrible as their actions may be, a la *The Godfather*, when it came to family they were wonderful. It was that same thought process that brought us to this season. We were always pretty good at fleshing out some of our bad guys, and getting away from the moustache twirling Dr Evil, to base them in reality. But I don't think we ever did it as well as we did in season four with

Shohreh [Dina Araz], who was a miracle find for us. She is an incredible actress, and I thought her family was too. Nestor [Serrano] did a great job as the husband and Jonathan [Ahdout] was just wonderful as her son. The connection between all three of them was so great. I remember shooting the very first scene with them sitting at the kitchen table arguing about family stuff, it wasn't even about them being terrorists, and we are watching the carnage of the train wreck they cause as they are sitting there calmly eating breakfast. I remember turning to someone saying, 'I've done a lot of scary stuff on this show over four years, but that is one of the scariest scenes I have ever shot.' I thought that at the time, because you think this could be my neighbor or the guy down the street. To me, that is much scarier than a nuclear bomb hitting LA, because you can't get your head around that."

Research Files

Sensory Disorientation: Richard Heller also undergoes sensory disorientation torture at CTU. Known as sensory deprivation, it is a technique used in psychological experimentation, torture and alternative medicine. A person is placed in isolation and one or more of the subject's five senses are deprived of stimuli. There are simple ways to engage in the practice, such as with blindfolds or acoustic earmuffs. In more elaborate examples, the subject can be subjected to machines that subtract the sense of smell, touch, 'gravity', taste and heat. While some people respond well to these tactics in the short-term, even being relaxed, long-term exposure can be extremely uncomfortable, causing anxiety, hallucinations, depression, and antisocial behavior. In modern times, the UK used five deprivation techniques when interrogating Irish suspects, which included wall-standing, hooding, subjection to noise, deprivation of sleep, and deprivation of food and drink.

Additional Intel

Production designer Joseph Hodges not only designs the large-scale sets for *24*, he is also responsible for designing all the ID badges, graphics and props.

10:00 am – 11:00 am

Director: Brad Turner
Writer: Stephen Kronish

Guest Cast: Louis Lombardi (Edgar Stiles), Shohreh Aghdashloo (Dina Araz), Angela Goethals (Maya Driscoll), Alex Skuby (Sergeant Dennis McGrath)

"I expect you to be able to walk and chew gum at the same time, Sarah." *Erin Driscoll*

Timeframe	Key Events

10:01 A.M. Driscoll is livid at Jack and sends tactical to find him.

10:03 A.M. Jack takes Kalil's gun.

10:05 A.M. Jack calls Chloe. She is called into a meeting and logs off.

10:07 A.M. Driscoll has Sarah bug Chloe.

10:08 A.M. Omar is frustrated that Kalil has gone silent. He boots up the routers. Heller's heart condition acts up.

10:14 A.M. Chloe admits to Edgar she is helping Jack and asks him to do the satellite tracking because she is being bugged. He agrees. Marianne hears it all.

10:16 A.M. Heller fakes a heart attack. He and Audrey overcome the guard, but Omar catches them.

10:19 A.M. Kalil tries to overcome Jack with bug spray. A cop arrives. Jacks locks everyone in the freezer.

10:26 A.M. Dina questions Debbie and serves her iced tea.

10:28 A.M. Dina calls Navi. He says Behrooz must clean up his problem.

10:30 A.M. Chloe comes up clean, but Driscoll makes Sarah figure out who else is helping.

10:32 A.M. Driscoll's troubled daughter Maya calls.

10:34 A.M. Dina hands Behrooz a gun.

10:39 A.M. Behrooz tells Debbie to run, but she collapses – drugged by Dina.

10:42 A.M. Police arrive and Jack threatens to tear gas everyone.

10:44 A.M. Chloe calls Jack with satellite tracking. Jack grabs Kalil at gunpoint and together they get in a car.

10:46 A.M. Jack lets Kalil go, while Chloe tracks him and downloads to Jack's PDA.

10:52 A.M. A call about Maya has Driscoll abuse her position to get her daughter back to the CTU clinic.

10:54 A.M. Curtis finds Jack. Driscoll arrests Chloe and sends a team to get Kalil.

10:56 A.M. Kalil calls Omar.

10:57 A.M. Marianne blackmails Edgar. Sarah plays Kalil's call back and they realize Jack was right.

10:58 A.M. Jack is stopped by a police blockade.

Heller takes action.

Debbie dies in Behrooz's arms.

The police catch up with Jack.

Iranian born actress Shohreh Aghdashloo was offered the role of the matriarch of the clandestine terrorist family, Dina Araz. Very selective about taking Middle Eastern roles portraying her heritage negatively, the *24* producers had to sell the actress on the part. Casting director Debi Manwiller says, "Shohreh was a big get. She is really well respected and a symbol in her community and we are asking her to play a terrorist! But she talked to her teenage daughter and she said that she should do it. Shohreh then watched episodes and talked to the producers." Peggy Kennedy continues, "One of the things the guys did make very clear was that she was a terrorist, but that she wouldn't be stereotypical." Manwiller adds, "Once she got here, she enjoyed it and relished it. I just can't imagine anyone else to play that role."

Once she slipped into the character, Aghdashloo says she

trusted the writers and only offered a few suggestions. "The only thing I wanted to enforce was during an episode directed by Jon Cassar," she remembers. "I wanted to bring in a lot of Casablanca lilies for the scene where I have to kill my son's girlfriend. I am so glad that Jon Cassar accepted it and he liked the idea very much. I wanted [Dina] to be very humanistic at the time that she acts animalistic. I needed that contradiction. The woman who is preparing white lilies, you think that she is expecting her lover to arrive at any minute. You wouldn't think she was preparing to kill her son's girlfriend. I love that. There is also a stillness that I used in that scene. Dina is coming down the stairs and she is totally one hundred percent in stillness. I needed that stillness in that scene. It wasn't easy and it came hard, it was challenging."

Research Files

Nitroglycerin: Heller fakes a heart attack to get his captors to bring him his nitroglycerin pills. For 130 years, nitroglycerin has been used to treat patients with angina and heart failure. When ingested it works as a vasodilator, opening up the constricted coronary arteries. In a relatively short period of time, the patient's chest pain will subside, blood pressure will decrease and their heart rate will increase. A few drawbacks to the use of nitroglycerin are that patients develop a resistance and sometimes even an addiction to it after prolonged use. Withdrawal headaches can be so severe that morphine-based medications are necessary to counteract the pain.

Additional Intel

Aghdashloo says she suggested using Puccini's opera *Madame Butterfly* for this episode, but they couldn't acquire the legal rights to it. Composer Sean Callery did compose an operatic-inspired score that the actress loved.

11:00 am - 12:00 pm

Director: Jon Cassar
Writer: Peter M. Lenkov

Guest Cast: Nestor Serrano (Navi Araz), Aisha Tyler (Marianne Taylor), Tony Plana (Omar), Angela Goethals (Maya Driscoll), Shohreh Aghdashloo (Dina Araz), Anil Kumar (Kalil Hasan)

"You're a geek, Edgar, but you are a good guy. Stay that way." Chloe O'Brian

Timeframe	Key Events

11:00 A.M. Edgar tracks Kalil. The police call Driscoll about Jack. She allows him to follow Kalil.

11:04 A.M. Edgar taps into Kalil's phone. Omar confirms Audrey is alive and Heller signed.

11:06 A.M. Heller asks Audrey to choke him to death. She refuses but knocks a gas pipe open to kill them both.

11:14 A.M. Marianne demands Edgar help her or she will tell Driscoll he helped Chloe. He relents.

11:16 A.M. Driscoll tells Jack that Chloe is suspended. She then asks Chloe to resign. She agrees.

11:18 A.M. Dina shoots Debbie's body to cover for Behrooz.

11:21 A.M. Marianne gets clearance.

11:22 A.M. Chloe is escorted out, but tells Edgar she didn't implicate him.

11:28 A.M. Kalil is pulled over by a cop. Panicked, Jack radios to release Kalil immediately.

11:33 A.M. Kalil calls Omar and is suspicious he was let go. Kalil drives himself into a truck.

11:39 A.M. Jack calls CTU and has them do a thermal scan of the perimeter.

11:41 A.M. Driscoll goes to find Maya. Curtis confronts Marianne.

11:44 A.M. Omar calls Navi, who is concerned about the broadcast.

11:45 A.M. Audrey and Heller are out cold in the cell. Omar revives them and Audrey recognizes a man named Gelfand.

11:46 A.M. Edgar finds the compound for Jack.

11:47 A.M. President Keeler's aide, Robert Franklin, suggests a preemptive strike on the compound to save the administration embarrassment.

11:53 A.M. Debbie's mom arrives at the Araz's.

11:57 A.M. Curtis tells Jack the President's only priority is Heller.

11:58 A.M. Omar begins the trial. The President orders the strike.

11:59 A.M. Jack goes in for Heller and Audrey.

Edgar says goodbye to Chloe.

Kalil becomes a martyr.

President Keeler orders the strike.

Curtis Manning was introduced early in the season as the Assistant Director of Field Operations of LA CTU and was then quickly promoted to Director after Ronnie Lobell was killed. Throughout the season, Manning became Jack's unofficial field partner – a trustworthy balance to Bauer's unorthodox ways. Actor Roger Cross explains his early assessment of Manning: "Initially, I thought of him as being a guy who has been through a lot of things and he's probably been in different branches of the military before coming to CTU. I chose to make it that he is one of those guys that still works for the government because he believes in truth and justice and helping to save the American people. I did make those decisions on my own and brought it to the group as the character and they liked how it fit and I'm still here," he chuckles.

Not long after his introduction at CTU, Manning's former

love affair with fellow CTU analyst Marianne Taylor (Aisha Taylor) was exposed as well. Cross says the producers gave him a heads up about the storyline. "Joel [Surnow] told me they were going to give me some fun stuff to do and that they were casting a lady to be my love interest. They asked if I wanted to sit in on the auditions to see or meet some of the people. It worked out better that they didn't see me in there and I trusted them to make those choices. It worked out beautifully and Aisha did a great job. I thought we had great chemistry together. We were always cracking jokes. It was a love/love thing and we get along great. It was fun to laugh and to tease each other and still be able to pull off the great chemistry between these two people... even when she tried to get me killed!"

Research Files

Thermal Scan: Jack has CTU do a thermal scan of the perimeter of the compound. Thermal imaging is an infrared process that detects radiation and with a video camera can reproduce the images of the radiation in the shape of what is emitting it. The amount of radiation emitted by an object increases with the temperature, thus thermal images and scans will capture the variations clearly. Humans and other warm-blooded animals become easily visible against the environment in the day or night, which makes it an effective tool for military and security branches that need to locate hidden individuals or life forms in difficult visual situations.

Additional Intel

Debbie's cell phone caller ID reflects the number: 310-597-3781. The number is real and during season four connected fans to *24* cast and crew, like Carlos Bernard and Kim Raver. Director Jon Cassar created the 'Fan Phone', as a thank you to the audience.

12:00 pm - 1:00 pm

Director: Jon Cassar
Writer: Matt Michnovetz

Guest Cast: Jonathan Ahdout (Behrooz Araz), James Frain (Paul Raines), Tony Plana (Omar), Shohreh Aghdashloo (Dina Araz), René Millán (Tariq)

"Living here has changed him. He has been like a stranger to us. He proved it to me today that he no longer believes in our cause. Maybe... he never did." *Navi Araz*

Timeframe

12:00 P.M. Jack enters the compound. He has seven minutes before the strike.

12:05 P.M. Jack finds Audrey and gives her a knife. He goes after Heller.

12:06 P.M. Jack finds Heller and saves him at the last second. Omar escapes. Keeler calls off the strike. Audrey is missing.

12:08 P.M. Heller and Jack escape. Gunfire erupts. A US Marine Cobra helicopter arrives and Marines rappel down.

12:11 P.M. Omar comes out with Audrey, who knifes her captor in the leg. Jack knifes Omar, who releases Audrey. The Marines shoot him dead.

12:17 P.M. Audrey tells Jack she can ID the man with Omar. Audrey's husband calls from CTU.

12:21 P.M. Navi tells Behrooz that Heller's trial is only part one. Tariq arrives to help with Debbie's body.

12:27 P.M. Curtis finds the briefcase with an 'MF' logo.

12:28 P.M. At CTU, Heller asks Audrey if Paul knows about her relationship with Jack. She is surprised.

12:30 P.M. The briefcase is tracked to a defense contractor who will only talk with DoD clearance. Heller helps.

12:31 P.M. Dina arrives home to a troubled Navi. He says Behrooz is with Tariq. Dina knows Behrooz will be killed. Navi says it's Marwan's wishes.

12:38 P.M. Heller commends Driscoll and Jack remains quiet. Driscoll asks Jack to be the temp head of field ops for the crisis.

12:44 P.M. Tariq drives Behrooz out to the mountains.

12:45 P.M. Paul asks Audrey to come back to him.

12:55 P.M. Behrooz confronts Tariq, who says Navi ordered it. Behrooz kills him with a shovel.

12:57 P.M. CTU determines the briefcase held a device to override or melt down a nuclear power plant.

12:59 P.M. Marianne calls someone to say that CTU has discovered the override.

Key Events

Omar takes Audrey hostage.

The love triangle...

Behrooz learns the truth about Navi.

In the climactic scene where Omar holds Audrey at gunpoint, actress Kim Raver says she was proud that her character remained strong. "What I loved about Audrey was that she wasn't just a victim and she had that in her in the fourth season and it really came to fruition in the fifth season. When she and her father try to escape... that was great. But I also love the moment where she is coming out [of the building with Omar] and Jack gives her that look and she jabs the guy in the leg [with the knife]. It's just so awesome! I love that because it shows the connection between her and Jack. There is that look between the two of them right before that kind of says go ahead with the knife and then he shoots him. There is no doubt in her mind that Jack is taking her through it, when to go and when to do it. There is an amazing connection between them and this faith that Jack will get her through."

Raver admits that the chemistry between Audrey and Jack was incredible to play and the tender, small moments really defined the depth of their love. "You can see throughout the fourth season, there are little things, like after Jack rescues Audrey, there is a great conversation where she is looking at Jack and Paul calls. Sure there are definitely feelings and she is shocked that Paul is in Los Angeles. No one knows that Jack and Audrey are an item, not even my father, but after I hang up the phone and walk by him, there is this amazing moment where Jack and Audrey grab hands. It shows these amazing feelings of needing and wanting to be together. It's what life is about – it's complicated. I think *24* captures that in an amazing way. While the thing of the day is happening, we are all trying to rectify whatever the terrorists are doing, but we also have our lives. Jack with his daughter, and me and Jack, and me and my ex-husband. What is so interesting are the interpersonal relationships and who becomes what kind of person on that day."

Research Files

Cobra Helicopter: The US Marines arrive at the compound where James Heller and Audrey Raines are being held in a Cobra helicopter. An attack helicopter, this particular model has a long history in US combat dating back to Vietnam. The current AH-1 model is a fixture in the Iraq War and it can travel up to 120 mph. Designed with a narrow front to make it harder for enemies to acquire it as a target, the Cobra is the primary helicopter used by the US Marines. Its main strength is going up against armored targets. The model is well known in popular culture as it was prominently featured in the animated *G.I. Joe* series, and for decades on film in movies such as *Iron Eagle, Courage Under Fire, War of the Worlds* and *Mission: Impossible III*.

Additional Intel

Editor Scott Powell says that the editing style of *24* has changed over time. Season one had a much slower pace with a lot of dialogue, while season four shifted to more action and quick cuts.

Navi Araz

Nationality:

Naturalized US Citizen

Experience:

No criminal record.
Owner of electronics store in Carso, CA

Expertise:

Proficiency in fixing computers, televisions

Personal:

Married - Dina Araz
Son - Behrooz Araz

Dina Araz

Nationality:

Emigrated to the United States 5 years ago.
Became a naturalized US citizen 2 years later.

Experience:

No criminal record.
Housewife and mother - West Valley, CA

Personal:

Married - Navi Araz
Son - Behrooz Araz

1:00 pm – 2:00 pm

Director: Ken Girotti

Writers: Joel Surnow & Michael Loceff

Guest Cast: Arnold Vosloo (Habib Marwan), Nestor Serrano (Navi Araz), Aisha Tyler (Marianne Taylor), Angela Goethals (Maya Driscoll)

> "Contact Bauer. Either he finds the people responsible for planning the override, or we're looking at a nuclear holocaust." Secretary of Defense James Heller

Timeframe

1:00 P.M. Jack and Audrey go to the security firm.

1:03 P.M. CTU assesses the meltdown could occur in three hours.

1:06 P.M. Paul confronts Jack about Audrey.

1:07 P.M. Marianne finds out where Jack is going.

1:10 P.M. Behrooz calls Dina. She promises to pick him up. Dina confronts Navi.

1:17 P.M. Audrey tells Jack she is divorcing Paul.

1:19 P.M. Marwan calls Navi, who lies and says Tariq killed Behrooz.

1:20 P.M. Edgar comes up with code that will stop the Dobson Override device, but the process could set off a chain nuclear reaction.

1:29 P.M. Driscoll stops in to check on Maya.

1:31 P.M. Richard passes the sensory technique and refuses to speak to his father again.

1:33 P.M. Dina meets Behrooz and tries to get him to leave on a train. She is shot in the arm. Behrooz escapes from Navi by car.

1:40 P.M. Navi faces Marwan. He asks permission to look for Dina at local hospitals. Marwan says Navi will pay for his failure.

1:42 P.M. Jack reaches the security company. Marianne calls Jack requesting the suspect's name.

1:43 P.M. Driscoll is dismayed to see Maya given Haldol, which she is allergic to.

1:45 P.M. Audrey is able to make the ID. Two men burst in firing, but Jack kills them. He downloads the footage onto memory sticks. CTU has been compromised.

1:53 P.M. Heller debriefs the President on the reactors.

1:55 P.M. Jack and Audrey are cornered in the garage. Tony Almeida comes out firing and saves them.

1:57 P.M. Edgar works the code and manages to shut down all but six reactors. The Dobson Device has corrupted those and meltdown is imminent.

Key Events

Driscoll's daughter has a reaction.

Marwan is revealed.

Tony Almeida to the rescue!

Matt Michnovetz joined *24* in season four as a staff writer, with episode number six serving as his début script. "It was the episode where Jack rescues Secretary of Defense Heller and his daughter, Audrey, from the terrorists at the compound. It was a big one. There was a lot of action and we went through a lot of drafts on that script. I did a few of the first drafts all by myself, but I was nervous and new to TV. Howard and the guys came in and rewrote me a couple times, but they allowed me to come back and do a couple of scenes. The general story is very similar to how we broke it, so the concept stayed the same, but the actual orchestration of the scenes and the dialogue changed considerably from first draft to final draft, which is usually the case. It's regular for this show for everybody to get rewritten."

As a new writer to television and the series, Michnovetz says

he was amazed by how inclusive the producers were with him throughout the season, allowing him to pitch ideas that became big moments in the year. "In episode eight, I got a story credit. I sort of pushed myself into the room when Stephen Kronish and Peter Lenkov were writing one of their episodes and they were gracious enough to give me a story credit because I gave them a couple of ideas. I was blown away by the episode they wrote. It's the one where Jack pulls Tony off the sidelines. There was some great chemistry between them and a lot of emotion. I also contributed to the idea of hijacking a stealth fighter to use on the President." Now a story editor on *24*, Michnovetz sheepishly admits he has since earned the title of 'Human Encyclopedia of *24*'. "There are a couple of things I am good at, and retaining *24* knowledge is one of them."

Research Files

Meltdown: A nuclear meltdown occurs when the core of a nuclear reactor fails to properly cool and the fuel assemblies, filled with plutonium, uranium and fission by-products, overheat and literally melt. A meltdown is considered a massive failure of the system because of the breach in containment of the radiation, which is released into the immediate area near the reactor. Current nuclear reactor designs and safety implementations make meltdown scenarios far more rare, with new containment structures able to thwart leaks like those that have occurred previously in history. Two of the largest nuclear meltdowns include the Russian Chernobyl disaster in 1986 and the Three-Mile Island meltdown in the United States in 1979.

Additional Intel

In 2006, Japanese action figure company Medicom created two Jack Bauer figures based on season four. Bauer wearing a vest is based on the episode 11 am – 12 pm and Bauer wearing his DOD suit is from episode 7 am – 8 am.

2.00 pm – 3.00 pm

Director: Ken Girotti
Story: Matt Michnovetz
Teleplay: Stephen Kronish & Peter M. Lenkov

Guest Cast: Carlos Bernard (Tony Almeida), Jonathan Ahdout (Behrooz Araz), Louis Lombardi (Edgar Stiles), David Newsom (Scott Borman), Roxanne Day (Jen Slater)

"Jack, it'd be pretty stupid of me to let you die right after I risked my life trying to save you." Tony Almeida

Timeframe

Key Events

2:00 P.M. Keeler is debriefed.

2:03 P.M. Jack calls Heller about the CTU mole.

2:05 P.M. Tony explains Michelle divorced him and he recently got out of prison because of Jack and Palmer.

2:06 P.M. Keeler tells the nation of the threat.

2:07 P.M. Marwan says he will operate the Override.

2:08 P.M. Behrooz begs his mother to go to the hospital.

2:09 P.M. Marianne calls Powell about the security breach. He orders her to stay at CTU.

2:10 P.M. Heller's assistant, Scott, arrives at CTU. Heller tells him to lie to Driscoll about where Jack is and put a Defense Department Comsat envelope on CTU.

2:16 P.M. At Tony's home, they upload the Felsted data to his computer.

2:21 P.M. The video is sent to Jack's DC office.

2:23 P.M. Despite her protests Sarah is arrested for passing classified information.

2:29 P.M. Edgar doesn't believe it is Sarah and researches her system.

2:30 P.M. Driscoll brings in the torture specialist who tasers Sarah.

2:43 P.M. DoD calls Jack and confirms the man is Powell, a consultant on the Override device. Powell is attempting to flee by helicopter.

2:44 P.M. Jack calls Driscoll. Tony offers to assist him.

2:46 P.M. Behrooz grabs Dina and they flee the hospital.

2:52 P.M. Edgar sets up Marianne so he can monitor her transmissions.

2:55 P.M. Edgar tells Curtis and Driscoll about Marianne.

2:56 P.M. Curtis stops Marianne from escaping. Her car is impounded, but it blows up and knocks her unconscious.

2:57 P.M. Powell's pilot tells them they are grounded. Powell pulls a gun.

2:58 P.M. Jack and Tony get Powell. A sniper shot fires and kills Powell.

Sarah gets tortured.

Marianne's car goes boom!

Powell gets taken out.

Production designer Joseph Hodges was given the opportunity to completely rebuild the massive CTU set for season four. The entire production moved from Woodland Hills to Chatsworth during the break between seasons three and four, which afforded Hodges the opportunity to start from scratch on a much sleeker, high-tech looking CTU. "The first set lasted for three years and I got very, very bored with it," Hodges laughs. "Joel [Surnow] originally said we were just going to build CTU as we had done, so I went to his office and got down on my knees and said, 'Please let me design something new!' So they said, 'Yeah, sure.'"

In Hodge's office is his very futuristic, curved desk that he says was part of his inspiration for the new CTU set. "It was a combination of two things. I actually built my desk for my house. I did the desk first and then I saw a building near here

and I decided to design the whole of CTU around the concept of curves. The original CTU never had a great exterior because it was so far to go to the building where they originally shot it and it didn't have any presence. Around the corner from here, there is this lovely building that has these two huge curved feet. I thought because it was only around the corner, we could shoot it and use it as the exterior. I wanted CTU to be a character. It's not just an office building. It's this cool space that ventures on the fantasy, but it still feels real. Some people joke about it having skateboard ramps, but to me there is no angle in there that isn't a beautiful shot. The CTU set, because it pushes the limits of an office, is one of my favorites."

Research Files

Reporting Gunshot Wounds: When Dina Araz enters the hospital, she tells doctors she was injured on a nail rather than shot by a gun. Almost all fifty states have laws that require healthcare providers to report injuries that are sustained through firearms. Doctors can be charged with a criminal offense if they do not report treating a gunshot victim within twenty-four hours. The debate about this subject rages on continually as doctors and law enforcement have differing opinions as to which is more important — the safety and privacy of a patient or the public disclosure that could prevent more injury to other people or help in the arrest of a criminal.

Additional Intel

The Council on American Islamic Relations was very unhappy with the portrayal of the Araz family, so during this episode Kiefer Sutherland addressed their protests by appearing in a public service announcement that reiterated the fictional nature of the show.

3:00 pm 4:00 pm

Director: Brad Turner
Writers: Howard Gordon & Evan Katz

Guest Cast: Shohreh Aghdashloo (Dina Araz), Cameron Bancroft (Lee Castle), Carlos Bernard (Tony Almeida), Louis Lombardi (Edgar Stiles), Nancy Linehan Charles (Lucy Stiles)

"No one is innocent." Dina Araz

Timeframe	Key Events

3:03 P.M. Keeler grills Heller about Marianne. The San Gabriel Island reactor will melt down in the hour.

3:04 P.M. Jack has Edgar trace calls on Powell's cell.

3:07 P.M. Dina's cell rings, which is being traced by Edgar. He PDAs the location to Jack.

3:09 P.M. Behrooz offers to get Dina's brother at the hospital.

3:11 P.M. Driscoll tells Heller San Gabriel is in meltdown.

3:16 P.M. Edgar calls his housebound mother who lives near the reactor.

3:18 P.M. Audrey offers to coordinate the National Guard.

3:20 P.M. Jack and agents raid the motel. Jack stops Dina before she commits suicide.

3:23 P.M. Behrooz asks his Uncle Naseem to give him pain pills for his mother. Naseem calls Navi, who demands his son is kept there until he arrives.

3:29 P.M. Edgar begs Audrey for help with his mother.

3:30 P.M. Jack finds that Dina and Navi have no criminal records.

3:31 P.M. Driscoll plays Jack a taped message between mother and son. Jack figures out that Behrooz is his leverage.

3:33 P.M. Jack confronts Dina about Behrooz and Navi. He promises to get Behrooz a pardon if she helps them find the Override.

3:40 P.M. Keeler agrees to the pardon.

3:41 P.M. Audrey tells Edgar they couldn't get his mother.

3:42 P.M. Edgar talks one last time to his mother.

3:45 P.M. Dina calls Behrooz about the pardon. She and agents will pick him up.

3:47 P.M. Naseem admits he called Navi. Behrooz runs.

3:49 P.M. Behrooz runs into Navi. Naseem follows and Navi shoots him.

3:55 P.M. Jack and Tony arrive, but the Arazs are gone.

3:56 P.M. Navi throws Behrooz into his car.

3:57 P.M. Navi hits Jack, who is able to shoot the tires out.

3:58 P.M. Navi takes Behrooz at gunpoint and they escape through a door.

3:59 P.M. Dina says all the reactors will melt down in two hours and she is glad.

Dina tries to commit suicide.

Edgar and his mother say goodbye.

Navi is ready to kill Behrooz.

CTU has seen its share of quirky, odd and sometimes downright evil employees come and go over the years, but after Chloe O'Brian, certainly the most beloved by the audience is Senior Internet Protocol Manager Edgar Stiles. Introduced in season four, Stiles was a nerdy sad sack analyst with a lisp who became Chloe's sparring partner and eventually a tragic hero during the meltdown crisis. Character actor Louis Lombardi remembers how creator/executive producer Joel Surnow drafted him to work on *24*. "He said, 'I saw you in *The Sopranos* and I want to put you on my show in this role.' So [my agent and I] read the role breakdown and it was for a nerdy geeky computer guy. I said, 'This don't sound right to me!' But I went in and [Joel] put me in the role."

Cast in the recurring role, Lombardi shares, "I didn't expect them to use me as much. The whole first season I expected to

facilitate what Jack Bauer needed. You know, you are in a couple of scenes and you are the computer guy. So I didn't think that the fourth season was going to be as big as it was, but they just kept adding and adding and adding. And I did what they said. Their writing is unbelievable. That's what makes the show so good — so I ain't changing anything. Tell me what you want me to say and I said it. All I did was add my personality to it in a way that I gave life to their lines." The actor admits the highlight of the season came during this episode, where he lost his mother to the radiation. "The effort he made to try and save his mother. He was a hero. He really tried and tried. I was devastated. I watch it now and I cry how many years later? It's the saddest thing. You have this really sad person trying to save his mother from dying and she kills herself on the phone with him! It was incredible. When I read that I knew it was going to blow the character out of the water."

Research Files

National Guard: Audrey Raines works to coordinate the United States National Guard in the meltdown aftermath. The Guard is a component of the United States Army and the United States Air Force. The Militia Act of 1903 organized the various state militias into the National Guard system found in the US today. For decades, the National Guard motto was 'One weekend a month, two weeks a year', with soldiers serving part-time while they maintained other primary work. The President of the United States or the governor of an individual state can call up the Guard at any time to help regular armed forces in times of emergency. A recent example of their service is during the Hurricane Katrina disaster in 2005. The oldest military unit under the Guard in the country is the 182nd Infantry Regiment and 101st Engineer Battalion of the Massachusetts Army National Guard, which were first organized in 1636.

Additional Intel

Computer graphics supervisor Mark Marcum says the nuclear reactor storyline was one of the roughest for his team because the writers moved the location of the reactors after they had already shot the footage, so the maps didn't match exactly.

4:00 pm - 5:00 pm

Director: Brad Turner

Writers: Stephen Kronish & Peter M. Lenkov

Guest Cast: James Frain (Paul Raines), Louis Lombardi (Edgar Stiles), Nestor Serrano (Navi Araz), Aisha Tyler (Marianne Taylor), Arnold Vosloo (Habib Marwan)

> "I hardly hear from you for about six months, and then you see me with another man, and suddenly you're pouring Dom Perignon." Audrey Raines

Timeframe   Key Events

4:00 P.M. Jack briefs CTU and asks for a thermal SAT to scan for bodies.

4:03 P.M. Navi calls Marwan and tells him Dina is arrested and he has Behrooz. Marwan says he needs two hours to melt down the rest of the reactors.

4:04 P.M. The scan finds two bodies in the laundry room. Jack plans to rappel into the room.

4:05 P.M. Grieving, Edgar has to refocus to slow down the Override.

4:06 P.M. Powell's body is wheeled in to Marianne. She agrees to talk and reveals Powell's contacts are on his computer.

4:10 P.M. Jack has Dina call Navi to distract him.

4:11 P.M. A noise alerts Navi of Jack in the room. The two fight.

4:13 P.M. Navi is shot in the back by Behrooz.

4:14 P.M. Dina and Behrooz are reunited. She gives Jack an address in the Valley where the Override last was.

4:20 P.M. A recovering Sarah asks to go back to work.

4:21 P.M. Curtis puts a tracking chip on Marianne.

4:24 P.M. Jack, Tony and CTU raid the building at the address. It's empty except for schematics on the reactors and train.

4:31 P.M. Sarah determines Galaxy Financial owns the building.

4:32 P.M. CTU discovers the CEO of Galaxy is Paul Raines. Jack has Audrey call him.

4:35 P.M. Audrey lies to Paul about reconciling and asks to meet.

4:36 P.M. Jack asks Tony to take the Arazs to CTU.

4:42 P.M. Driscoll agrees with Tony being reinstated.

4:44 P.M. Curtis is briefed on Paul.

4:45 P.M. Heller calls Audrey, livid she is meeting Paul alone.

4:46 P.M. Driscoll orders Sarah to watch Tony. She demands a promotion and a clear record.

4:55 P.M. Marianne and Curtis are ambushed. She is killed and Curtis knocked unconscious.

4:57 P.M. Jack bursts into the hotel room and punches Paul.

Behrooz gets revenge on dad.

Marianne is expendable.

Jack confronts Paul.

The season-long arc charting the relationship between Jack and Audrey included every painful hurdle one could imagine, including kidnapping, returned estranged husbands, the brutality of the job and more. Co-executive producer and director Jon Cassar says despite all the agony, their story was always compelling. "The whole Jack romance with Audrey was very satisfying. It held over the whole year. The thought process in starting it was if there was one thing that was going to bring Jack back in, it would be his daughter. We didn't want to deal with that anymore as we had taken it as far as we could, so in came the romantic interest. Years before that, we had tried to introduce a romantic interest, because it's always nice to have in a story, but unfortunately because you are always dealing in real time, it was a drawback. We tried to do it in season two with Sarah Wynter, but there is so much priority to Jack

and he moves towards what is most important and that is saving American lives. Romance doesn't have a lot of chance to take hold. We even tried in season three with Claudia Salazar, but there was too much happening for it to root itself. Now, we've got a romance that has been going on for a year that is already established and very strong and very loving. It's away from the stress of CTU and saving the world. It's almost like being straight back to year one where you started with a romance with Teri [Bauer], his wife, which wasn't as strong as this one is because they were on the rocks. This one, to me, was even stronger than that relationship, so I knew and Kiefer knew this was the way to go. The other huge plus for us was getting Kim Raver. There just couldn't be a better match for Kiefer. There is a connection there that is real that comes through onscreen."

Research Files

Rappelling: When Jack tries to sneak up on Navi and Behrooz Araz, he chooses to rappel down a chute in order to surprise the two fugitives. Rappelling, or abseiling (which means 'to rope down'), is the act of descending down a fixed line. Jean Estéril Charlet, a Chamonix guide, is attributed with starting the practice back in 1876. There are many ways to rappel with the inclusion of descenders, proper rope and belays to ensure safety. While rappelling can be used strictly as a sport, it has also been incorporated into military, police and rescue operations, especially in environments where accessing injured people or accident sites is not possible due to the topography or dangerous materials.

Additional Intel

Production designer Joseph Hodges created the mobile camera Jack uses in the ductwork. "It was described like a little Jeep with a camera on it and I hated that so I fought with Joel about it. They said I had to make something, so I made a cool little car that looks like a stealth bomber, or like it could be a piece of the ductwork."

5:00 pm - 6:00 pm

Director: Jon Cassar

Writers: Joel Surnow & Michael Loceff

Guest Cast: Cameron Bancroft (Lee Castle), Angela Goethals (Maya Driscoll), Louis Lombardi (Edgar Stiles), James Frain (Paul Raines)

> "I give Behrooz about three months before he commits suicide. And you'll never hear word-one about what happens to him. Ever." Tony Almeida

Timeframe   Key Events

5:00 P.M. Jack zaps Paul with electricity, but he says he doesn't know the terrorists.

5:06 P.M. Marwan arrives at Powell's office, where he meets aide Ali.

5:08 P.M. Ali orders henchmen to kill Curtis. Curtis kills them with his bare hands, but he is locked in the building.

5:09 P.M. Paul finds Galaxy was taken over by Harris Barnes, an alias for Habib Marwan.

5:16 P.M. Tony threatens Behrooz unless Dina names names. She gives a few but doesn't ID Marwan.

5:19 P.M. Ali finds his dead men and searches for Curtis. Marwan orders all hard phone lines ripped out.

5:20 P.M. Driscoll is summoned to an upset Maya.

5:22 P.M. Paul apologizes to Audrey and they share a touch.

5:28 P.M. The names Dina gave Tony are all connected to Marwan.

5:29 P.M. Tony clears the interrogation room and tells Dina he will rip up the pardon so Behrooz will rot in jail. Terrified, she says Marwan was her cell contact. He has the Override.

5:32 P.M. Tony debriefs Jack and Driscoll. Meltdown two is a mere twenty minutes away.

5:34 P.M. Curtis overpowers a henchman for his phone and gun. He finds out the Override is upstairs. He contacts CTU.

5:36 P.M. Jack arrives and Curtis calls to direct him inside.

5:41 P.M. Driscoll's daughter is having a violent episode.

5:45 P.M. Jack and Curtis reconnect and determine the company Marwan is hiding inside to download the reactor virus.

5:54 P.M. Ali sees Jack and calls Marwan. The agents see Ali running and they fire. Marwan grabs a gun and fires in the air. Marwan runs and Jack follows. Curtis gets the Override.

5:56 P.M. Edgar is able to stop the Override and the meltdowns reverse.

5:58 P.M. Crisis averted, Driscoll goes to her daughter, who has killed herself.

5:59 P.M. Jack realizes Marwan is posing as a CTU agent.

Curtis takes out his captors.

Marwan causes a distraction.

Driscoll finds Maya dead.

In this episode, actor Roger Cross got to strut his action moves in a sequence where he takes out a room of Marwan's henchmen with his bare hands. "I definitely had some fun when they had the scene where I had to take the guys out," he laughs in remembrance. "They knew I had done some martial arts and wrestling, but they were like, 'Geez, you can really handle yourself!' So we worked it all out and that whole fight sequence was all me. My stunt double was there but he just ended up coordinating it. He did more things later, but at that time it was all me. They said they needed to get me out in the field more, so that was the birth of that. Before that, I was mainly in CTU, so from then I got the chance to get out there and stretch the legs and kick some butt, which was a lot of fun."

In his second season playing Curtis, Cross says the character is one he is proud to play because of the color-blind approach

of the producers. "It really kept me a fan of the show. The way that [Curtis] was written, I went in and did it and never once did [my race] become an issue. From the first time I went in and I met Joel Surnow, he said, 'I like what you did with that. Very natural.' I think I owe it to him because he created it," he chuckles. "That's what he is and I like that. I've always been a fan of that and the show lets people be people." Curtis has also become a role model for his community. "I hear that constantly," Cross says humbly. "Every time I hear it, I am happy, especially when I hear it from kids. It's nice. The show is a hit now and it's watched and it's a good feeling for me."

Research Files

Schizophrenia: Maya Driscoll suffers from an acute case of schizophrenia that eventually leads to her tragic suicide. Schizophrenia is roughly translated from Greek to mean, 'shattered mind', and is a psychiatric impairment that causes a person to have perception problems, including hallucinations, delusions and problems with cognitive thinking. There are many different symptoms that make up the diagnosis and some doctors believe it's actually an accumulation of several disorders clustered together. There are no biological tests to determine if someone has schizophrenia, but diagnosis usually comes from a psychiatric professional well versed in the symptoms. Treatment today relies on the use of antipsychotic medication, which cannot cure the condition but makes it manageable for the patient. In more extreme cases, hospitalization is the course of treatment, which can be voluntary or involuntary depending on the severity of the case.

Additional Intel

Evan Katz, co-writer of this episode, is a fan of the Australian band The Go-Betweens. He named the company McLennan-Forster after band members Grant McLennan and Robert Forster.

6:00 pm – 7:00 pm

Director: Jon Kassar

Writers: Howard Gordon & Evan Katz

Guest Cast: Angela Goethals (Maya Driscoll), Reiko Aylesworth (Michelle Dessler), Bill Smitrovich (Gene McLennan), Tomas Arana (Dave Conlon)

"More time? Edgar, since when do we have the luxury of time?" Sarah Gavin

Timeframe  Key Events

6:00 P.M. Edgar finds out Marwan works for McLennan-Forster.

6:02 P.M. Jack heads to the company HQ. Paul offers to go to help him access military files.

6:05 P.M. Driscoll refuses to give up command.

6:08 P.M. Marwan drops the CTU uniform and hops on a bus.

6:09 P.M. CTU is briefed on Marwan. Driscoll wanders out of the meeting. Sarah wants to report her.

6:10 P.M. Audrey returns to CTU to help Heller.

6:16 P.M. Driscoll passes out and is taken to medical. Heller makes Tony Interim Director of CTU Los Angeles.

6:19 P.M. Curtis and Sarah find Marwan had full security clearance at McLennan-Forster and weapons access.

6:20 P.M. CEO Gene McLennan is briefed on Marwan.

6:21 P.M. Head of security Dave Conlon meets Jack and Paul.

6:22 P.M. Another executive convinces McLennan to suppress information from CTU to save the company from ruin.

6:23 P.M. Executives tell Jack they will take their servers down to help CTU track Marwan.

6:31 P.M. Curtis is upset with Heller for appointing Tony.

6:32 P.M. Paul discovers many files have been deleted, which Conlon does in another room.

6:38 P.M. Driscoll leaves CTU.

6:41 P.M. Tony and Curtis clash, and Tony assures him he will be leaving by crisis end.

6:43 P.M. Marwan meets Yosik in an alley.

6:44 P.M. Paul rebuilds the deleted data. The executives panic and decide to detonate a pulse bomb.

6:52 P.M. Phones go down in the building. Paul prints out an encrypted file.

6:54 P.M. Jack discovers the EMP bomb and calls Tony.

6:55 P.M. Paul is threatened by Conlon, but Paul runs with the printout.

6:56 P.M. Jacks finds the EMP room and tries to stop it.

6:57 P.M. The blackout begins. Paul makes it outside but Conlon is there with his gun.

6:59 P.M. Driscoll's replacement from District arrives – Michelle Dessler.

Erin Driscoll leaves CTU.

Conlon finds Paul.

Michelle Dessler returns to CTU.

Costume designer Jim Lapidus and costume supervisor Jean Rosone reveal that one of their most challenging costume days came in season four with the Hazmat suits needed for the nuclear meltdown story arc. Lapidus was tasked to create a full body hazard suit that also provided a large window in the facial area to capture the actor's performances. "It wasn't a disaster, rather it was more of a win for me," Lapidus shares. "The day they shot it, it was 120 degrees in the Valley outside, with plastic covering the whole building. Nobody thought about Hazmat suits outside in the heat. I designed them to all have their own air systems, but I didn't sleep the night before thinking, 'What am I going to do? How are they going to work in this?' At the end of that day, I finally got back to the set because I had been out dressing everybody and I went up to Kiefer, because he had been in one of the suits, and I

Research Files

EMP Bomb: An electromagnetic bomb (or E-bomb) is a relatively new weapon and is an effective tool against today's technology. When an E-bomb is detonated, an electromagnetic shockwave emits short but intense waves which increase as they expand out and then quickly overwhelm electrical circuitry with an intense electromagnetic field. The fields then collide with electrical/electronic systems to produce damaging current and voltage surges that are passed from one component to the next, frying power sources, motherboards, batteries, wiring and transformers. While these bombs are not harmful to most humans, the widespread destruction of any electrical based materials can have significant impact on commerce, communications and other services dependent on technology. The only protection from such an attack is to wrap equipment in foil without any holes.

Additional Intel

Originally, the EMP bomb was written as a box with a blinking light on it, but production designer Joseph Hodges got creative and conceptualized it as a huge hexagonal box suspended in mid air to give more drama to the scene.

asked him, 'How was it?' He said, 'Jim, I was cooler inside the suit than I was outside the suit.' I was so panicked because of all that plastic covering this building, and in fact, the plastic made 120 degrees feel like 200 degrees. I was just so panicked. I don't like things like that. I don't like spacesuits or Hazmat suits because they are very uncomfortable and very hard to work with, but people tell me that this was probably one of the best ever designs I did in terms of functionality and comfort."

Jack Bauer

CTU Missions:

Team Leader – Operation Proteus
Section Captain – Hotel Los Angeles attack

Experience:

Department of Defense, Washington DC – Special Assistant to the Secretary of Defense
CTU – Director of Field Operations, Los Angeles Domestic Unit
CTU –Special Agent in Charge, Los Angeles Domestic Unit
Los Angeles PD – Special Weapons and Tactics

Education:

Basic SWAT School – LASD
University of California (Berkeley) – Master of Science, Criminology and Law
University of California (Los Angeles) – Bachelor of Arts, English Literature
Special Forces Operations Training Course

Military:

US Army – Combat Applications Group, Delta Force Counter Terrorist Group

Personal:

Widowed
Daughter – Kimberly Bauer

Audrey Raines

Experience:

Department of Defense, Washington DC – Senior Policy Analyst

Anderson Aerospace Corporation – Consultant for Government Contracts

Ballard Technology – Government Liaison

Registered Lobbyist

US Congress House Armed Services Committee – Legislative Assistant

Education:

Brown University – Master of Arts, Public Policy

Yale University – Bachelor of Arts, English

Personal:

Married – Paul Raines (separated)

7:00 pm - 8:00 pm

Director: Rodney Charters
Writer: Anne Cofell

Guest Cast: Carlos Bernard (Tony Almeida), Reiko Aylesworth (Michelle Dessler), Arnold Vosloo (Habib Marwan), Cameron Bancroft (Lee Castle), Tomas Arana (Dave Conlon)

> "The President of the United States is on a tight schedule. We can't be late." Habib Marwan

Timeframe | Key Events

7:00 P.M. All communications to Jack and Paul are down.

7:03 P.M. Conlon's guards beat Paul. Jack saves Paul and they retrieve the printout.

7:07 P.M. Michelle assigns Tony to research. He is livid. She gives him low-level clearance.

7:09 P.M. Curtis and Edgar surmise the company set off the EMP.

7:10 P.M. Marwan meets a man named Anderson, who says it will only take 30 minutes to get where he needs to go.

7:15 P.M. Sarah IDs a helicopter heading to McLennan-Forster.

7:16 P.M. Conlon instructs the helicopter mercenaries to erase Jack and Paul.

7:17 P.M. Jack helps Paul into a sporting goods store for weapons. Two Arab American owners are hiding from looters.

7:19 P.M. Jack plans to force the mercenaries to radio, which will tip off CTU. The owners say they will help.

7:26 P.M. Audrey admits to Heller that Jack torturing Paul disturbed her.

7:28 P.M. Sarah informs Michelle of her arrangement with Driscoll. They clash and Michelle has her escorted out of CTU.

7:31 P.M. Michelle assigns Tony with Curtis.

7:32 P.M. Tony and Michelle disagree on how to proceed, as Tony says he knows Jack's plan.

7:33 P.M. Jack fires a shot and the mercenarys radio for help.

7:44 P.M. Edgar sees the radio frequencies proving Tony's theory about Jack's plan.

7:45 P.M. Conlon gives the order to attack the store.

7:48 P.M. The mercenaries blow open the store and Edgar sees the gunfire has ceased.

7:54 P.M. Conlon enters and Jack takes him down.

7:55 P.M. SWAT arrives and the area is secured.

7:56 P.M. Tony confirms to Michelle Jack is safe. She apologizes and asks him to stay.

7:58 P.M. Conlon rises to shoot Jack in the back, but Paul takes the bullet.

7:59 P.M. Anderson in an Army uniform calls Marwan.

Fire fight in the sporting good store.

Paul takes a bullet for Jack.

Anderson gets into uniform.

By the middle of season four, audiences realized there was a different shift in the storytelling style for this season. The producers ended up tinkering with their format of creating three season-long arcs and instead just barreled through a series of disasters that kept the pace relentless. Co-creator and executive producer Robert Cochran explains their shock at finding how well the new dynamic worked. "I think it was a breakthrough for us to realize that in season four. It's not something we planned out, but we ended up scrambling and going from one thing to another. I think the sequence was that they steal a stealth fighter and they use it to shoot down Air Force One; then they get the Nuclear Football and use that to steal a missile; and then they put a nuclear weapon on the missile and fire it." Coexecutive producer Evan Katz chuckles, adding, "Heller was the camouflage for putting this virus in the system that melted

Night Vision Goggles: During the shootout at the sporting goods store, the mercenaries use night vision goggles to try and root out Jack and Paul in the dark. Now a standard piece of equipment in the military, there are two kinds of night vision goggles: passive and active. Active goggles project infrared light and create an image from the light reflected back. Passive goggles use a photo-electric effect, which draws in light and then amplifies it with an image intensifier. The intensifier boosts up a weakly lit image and allows it to become visible. The outcome with passive goggles is an image that has a green hue, chosen by developers because the human eye is able to perceive the most amount of shading in the color green. Night vision equipment is particularly sensitive to light, so major damage can occur to materials used in the daytime.

Additional Intel

While many fans (and even the country of Turkey) assumed that the Araz family was from Turkey, co-executive producer and director Jon Cassar dispels that notion, asserting that they purposefully never attributed a country of origin to them.

down a nuclear power plant and on and on and on and on. We were nervous about that, but Joel [Surnow] really urged that it would work and we couldn't stick to one threat. He was absolutely right. As long as we kept it interesting and had the connections be onscreen, it really worked. It was really a revelation for us and it freed us up to do more interesting seasons." Cochran concurs, adding, "If you actually think about all that happening in eight hours, please! But I think what happens is that, for the most part, the audience sees [the show] one week at a time and they don't think to themselves, "Hey, wait a minute! This can't happen in eight hours." They just see something neat."

8:00 pm - 9:00 pm

Director: Tim Iacofano
Writers: Howard Gordon & Evan Katz

Guest Cast: Louis Lombardi (Edgar Stiles), Geoff Pierson (President John Keeler), Arnold Vosloo (Habib Marwan), Shohreh Aghdashloo (Dina Araz)

> "I'm sick of people talking to me like I don't know what I'm doing — especially people who don't actually work here."
> Edgar Stiles

Timeframe

8:00 P.M. Paul is flown back to CTU.

8:03 P.M. Keeler secretly sets up a plan for martial law.

8:06 P.M. CTU determines a name from the file is a terrorist. Paul is taken to surgery.

8:07 P.M. Joseph Fayed is the suspect. Jack wants Dina to go undercover with him.

8:08 P.M. Marwan and Anderson meet.

8:09 P.M. An Air Force pilot is blackmailed and threatened by Marwan's associates.

8:10 P.M. Offering immunity for the Arazs, Dina agrees to take Jack as a hostage to Fayed.

8:17 P.M. Anderson enters the room with the pilot and takes him away.

8:21 P.M. Tony tells Michelle that Edgar is not focused.

8:22 P.M. Michelle gets Chloe to come back for the day to help Jack.

8:25 P.M. Jack allows Dina to see Behrooz.

8:32 P.M. Jack and Dina arrive and he gives her his gun.

8:33 P.M. Dina knocks and tells Fayed who she has. Fayed calls Marwan.

8:37 P.M. The Air Force pilot enters the base, with Anderson hiding in the collapsed backseat. Once inside, Anderson kills the pilot, takes his ID and snips his thumb off.

8:44 P.M. Paul has a bullet lodged near his spine and Audrey realizes she still loves him.

8:46 P.M. Fayed takes Jack and Dina to Marwan. Chloe has trouble with audio. Jack and Dina are put into another van.

8:48 P.M. CTU loses Jack and Dina, but they follow Fayed's car and stop him.

8:49 P.M. Fayed opens his briefcase and his car explodes.

8:56 P.M. Marwan accuses Dina of lying and tells her to kill Jack.

8:58 P.M. Dina aims and points at Marwan and clicks – no bullet. He orders Dina killed and takes Jack.

8:59 P.M. Anderson enters the high security area.

Key Events

Michelle gets Chloe back.

Dina turns on Marwan.

Marwan gets the ultimate revenge.

In this episode, Dina Araz meets her brutal end off screen in the shadows of a dark corridor, but actress Shohreh Aghdashloo says that wasn't always Dina's ultimate fate. "She wasn't supposed to die," she reveals. "I was told she was not going to die, but then they decided they were going to kill her. But I was happy with their decision because after all, it was their show." When Dina's death was finally written, Shohreh says she was given the script so she could prepare ahead of time. Laughing, the actress recounts, "This is really funny, because when they decided how I was going to get killed, I was supposed to take Jack Bauer to Marwan. When Marwan tells me that he knows that I am with them, I tell him, 'Believe me Marwan, I did not betray you.' Then he would immediately draw his gun and shoot me. So all weekend I read it and made myself ready. I bought myself knee bands because every time I

am dying [in a role], I try to come up with some truth in the matter of death. I always try to find some human way to die. At least a hundred times, I sort of tried to land on my knees and slowly and gradually fall... I was told that he would shoot me and I would fall to the ground into Jack Bauer's arms and look at him and, with my eyes, tell him, 'Take care of my son.' All weekend I tried it over and over again, a hundred different ways. The next day I went to work and before I even got to the set, Joel Surnow came to me and said, 'We are sorry, but we have changed the scene and I would like to let you know before you get to the scene. We aren't going to shoot you in front of the camera.' I said, 'Joel, I wish you had told me before this weekend! My knees are blue and black!'

Research Files

Mobile Parabolic: A parabolic microphone is used to collect sound from very specific points. Parabolic mics are usually situated on a stem with a concave reflector positioned right behind it to collect the sound and then focus it into the microphone receiver. The sound recordist points the mic in the direction of the sound they want to collect, and with a mobile parabolic, the operator can move closer to the sound to get clearer fidelity. Due to the nature of the parabolic and the collection of lots of sound, they aren't used for studio quality audio. Instead, they are often used to collect sound surreptitiously (i.e. eavesdropping) for law enforcement, or for sporting events and ambient nature sounds.

Additional Intel

The prop department holds thousands of prop pieces created and used for the series inside a chain link fenced area known as 'Area 51'. Set prop master Sterling Rush says the name is a play on the UFO Roswell mythology.

9:00 pm 10:00 pm

Director: Bryan Spicer
Writer: Joel Surnow and Michael Loceff

Guest Cast: Jonathan Ahdout (Behrooz Araz), Arnold Vosloo (Habib Marwan), Reiko Aylesworth (Michelle Dessler), Carlos Bernard (Tony Almeida), James Morrison (Bill Buchanan)

> "I was inappropriately blunt, wasn't I? Sorry… I do that a lot." Chloe O'Brian

Timeframe — Key Events

9:00 P.M. Dina's body is found.

9:03 P.M. Jack hears Marwan talking to Anderson, who is grounded. Marwan says their window is only an hour.

9:04 P.M. A mechanic tells Anderson the plane won't be fixed until morning. Anderson shoots him dead.

9:07 P.M. Marwan chains Jack and interrogates him.

9:09 P.M. A guard tells Marwan that police know about the missing pilot.

9:10 P.M. Marwan grills Jack about Behrooz.

9:12 P.M. Marwan calls CTU and is patched to Michelle. He wants to trade Jack for Behrooz.

9:18 P.M. Michelle has Curtis interrogate Behrooz.

9:19 P.M. Curtis summons the torture specialist for Behrooz.

9:20 P.M. Curtis gets physical with Behrooz. The syringe comes out and the boy screams.

9:22 P.M. Marwan calls Michelle with an exchange location.

9:23 P.M. The missing pilot report is sent to CTU.

9:24 P.M. Edgar passed the local missing person's report to a tech named Meg.

9:25 P.M. Anderson poses as the mechanic and says the delay was a false alarm. The flight is approved.

9:31 P.M. Meg alerts Chloe of the pilot, but Chloe passes it off to her "boss" Edgar.

9:33 P.M. Bill Buchanan from Division arrives. He is to oversee the prisoner exchange. Behrooz came up clean.

9:35 P.M. Anderson calls Marwan with the flight news.

9:41 P.M. Edgar is too busy to look at the pilot report.

9:43 P.M. Behrooz is told about the exchange and fitted with transmitters.

9:53 P.M. The CTU van arrives and Curtis walks Behrooz out.

9:54 P.M. Behrooz asks about Dina and Jack lies.

9:55 P.M. Once Behrooz is in the van, a sniper attempts to shoot Jack, but CTU snipers save the day.

9:57 P.M. Marwan's men tell Behrooz Dina is dead and take off his transmitters.

9:59 P.M. Anderson is ready to take off in a F-117A stealth fighter jet.

Curtis goes rough on Behrooz.

Bill Buchanan arrives at CTU.

Anderson pilots the stealth bomber.

By mid-season, with Erin Driscoll out mourning the death of her daughter and no one internally connecting the Los Angeles branch of CTU to Division, a new character was tossed into the fray to bring strong leadership back into the mix. Bill Buchanan strode purposefully into CTU without fanfare and immediately grounded the operations with what Howard Gordon calls Bill's "fast ball down the middle kind of leadership". Actor James Morrison remembers, "I showed up without introduction. I just sort of showed up. They didn't prepare anyone for my arrival. I suddenly showed up in the height of the kidnapping of Jack. For me as the character and the actor, it was like standing on the platform waiting for the train and it comes by at ninety miles per hour and doesn't stop. I just had to put my hand out and grab it and that's what it was like to come aboard at that level of intensity."

Research Files

F-117A: Mitch Anderson commandeers a Nighthawk to shoot down Air Force One. The elite stealth fighter is built by Lockheed and is the world's first aircraft designed specifically around stealth technology. The first flight of a Nighthawk was in 1977, but the US Air Force refused to acknowledge they existed until 1988, with its public unveiling occurring in 1990. Early on, due to the odd size and shape of the fighter, pilots nicknamed it 'cockroach', and it has stuck to this day. The F-117 was first used in combat during the invasion of Panama in 1989. Since then, the fleets of thirty-six combat-ready jets have been utilized extensively in Iraq conflicts and the Iraq war. With its sophisticated navigation systems, lack of radar and low emissions it is extremely effective at being difficult to track by enemy satellite.

Additional Intel

James Morrison has a varied career in the arts that includes acting, directing, and being a Yoga teacher. He began his acting career as a wirewalker and clown in the circus. Since then he's won a Los Angeles Drama Critics Circle Award, written and directed the short film *Parking* and published a book of prose and poetry called *Fog Slow To Clear*.

A longtime TV and theater veteran, Morrison reveals he almost wasn't able to take the role of Buchanan due to a conflict with another project. "I got the call to audition the day I was supposed to go on my Christmas vacation in Hawaii with my family. My manager talked me into staying for it because I didn't know the show. So I watched the episode where Jack shoots Chappelle and I just said, 'Oh my God, I've got to be on this show!' I auditioned the next day and didn't hear back for another two weeks. I was the choice for the role but Fox wouldn't let me do it because I was a recurring character on *Point Pleasant*. My manager wrote this brilliant letter and Joel [Surnow] and casting got hold of it and they let me have the role. So it turned out great and it was meant to be."

10:00 pm - 11:00 pm

Director: Ian Toynton
Story: Robert Cochran
Teleplay: Howard Gordon & Evan Katz

Guest Cast: Arnold Vosloo (Habib Marwan), James Frain (Paul Raines), Geoff Pierson (President John Keeler), Gregory Itzin (Vice President Charles Logan), James Morrison (Bill Buchanan)

"We're being beaten by our own technology."
Chloe O'Brian

Timeframe   Key Events

10:00 P.M. Keeler is debriefed and wants to land in LA.

10:03 P.M. Audrey tells Jack that Paul will recover.

10:05 P.M. Marwan tries to track down a backup hard drive with their plans.

10:08 P.M. Jack and agents raid the compound. Marwan runs. Jack finds a computer that is self-deleting.

10:10 P.M. Jack sees a red light and orders SWAT to evacuate. All the computers explode.

10:12 P.M. Marwan escapes.

10:16 P.M. The surgeon tells Audrey that Paul is paralyzed from the waist down.

10:19 P.M. Buchanan yells at Michelle for losing Marwan.

10:20 P.M. Jack sends some false passports to CTU for matches. Buchanan apologizes to Michelle tenderly. Tony gets jealous.

10:21 P.M. Michelle tells Jack they have a match on Anderson, a hired mercenary.

10:28 P.M. Marwan hides until a car picks him up.

10:29 P.M. On Air Force One, Keeler asks his teenage son to help him with his speech.

10:39 P.M. Tony confronts a startled Michelle about Buchanan.

10:42 P.M. At Anderson's apartment, an agent finds the hard drive in an electrical outlet. One of Marwan's people posing as an agent, Nicole, kills the real agent and takes the drive. Jack shoots her dead.

10:46 P.M. Jack gets Edgar to help him unlock the data. It's the schematics for a stealth bomber, which Anderson might be able to fly.

10:52 P.M. Tony finds out a bomber pilot never reported in. Air Force One prepares to land.

10:53 P.M. Michelle calls the President and he calls the Vice-President.

10:57 P.M. CTU is able to patch Jack through to Anderson. Jack begs the pilot to stop.

10:58 P.M. Keeler tells VP Charles Logan to stay the course if he dies.

10:59 P.M. Anderson fires on Air Force One, which breaks into pieces over the desert.

Paul is paralyzed.

Keeler says goodbye to his son.

Air Force One is hit.

Director and producer Brad Turner explains that the key to directing on *24* is never forgetting one core conceit – Jack Bauer may be an incredible hero, but he is very human. "It's all about keeping your eye on the ball with this show. You can get too lost in the style and not involved enough in the content. It's really easy to get distracted by style on this show and both Jon [Cassar] and I focus on the content. What are Jack Bauer's intentions? The toughest part is when you are into the action beats – you can't disregard the narrative. Kiefer is so involved in asking, 'What would I do in this situation if this was really me?' It's not a character that is a superhero, it's a guy doing this stuff, and we have to remember that because it's so easy to slide into superhero mode with this show. In reality, in a twenty-four-hour period, no one could do this, but you never want to lose the fact that it's a human being portrayed doing this. It's a

kind of a catch-22. We write a show that is humanly impossible to do, but on the other hand we want to portray it, and this is where we have been really successful, because people really believe this guy exists. He's not Spider-Man – if a bullet hits Jack, he bleeds. They know he is going to avoid it and somehow get away from it, but it's within the realm of human possibility that he does everything. I don't think anybody that watches the show is under the impression that that wouldn't happen to Jack Bauer. He pants and breathes and sweats and climbs out of every hole we put him in. It's something that is really hard to keep track of all the time, and that's important to our show, and that everything we do is believable. We can invent these impossible situations and somehow get out of them and move on to the next thing. We do it week in and week out."

Research Files

Spinal Injuries: When Paul takes a bullet for Jack, it lodges near his spinal cord causing paralysis. The two major reasons for spinal injuries are trauma and disease. Car accidents, gunshots, sporting injuries, or major falls are all common reasons for spinal trauma. It is a common misconception that the spinal cord has to be completely severed for loss of mobility to occur. In the United States, more than 450,000 people live with spinal injuries, with about 11,000 new injuries a year. Seventy-eight percent of spinal injuries occur in men aged sixteen to thirty. There are different levels of injury classified as complete injury or incomplete injury. Complete injury means there is no function below the line of injury. An incomplete injury means there is variable sensation based on the severity of damage to the area affected. Any patient with a spinal injury will have to participate in physical therapy to keep the mobile areas of the body in good condition and to prevent atrophy of areas that can't be voluntarily controlled.

Additional Intel

Kiefer Sutherland is the name the actor goes by in all his official television and film credits, but he actually has a much longer birth name that is officially Kiefer William Frederick Dempsey George Rufus Sutherland.

11:00 pm - 12:00 am

Director: Jon Cassar
Writer: Duppy Demetrius

Guest Cast: Jude Ciccolella (Mike Novick), Gregory Itzin (President Charles Logan), Louis Lombardi (Edgar Stiles), James Morrison (Bill Buchanan), John Allen Nelson (Walt Cummings)

"Marwan gave up the Football for his freedom."
Tony Almeida

Timeframe	Key Events

11:00 P.M. The pilot radios a distress call. Jack arrives at CTU.

11:05 P.M. Mike Novick prepares Logan to be sworn in.

11:07 P.M. Heller wants Jack to lead the team to recover the Nuclear Football, which has a tracer on it.

11:09 P.M. A couple, Jason and Kelly, camping in the desert sees the wreckage falling.

11:15 P.M. Buchanan confronts a hostile Tony and admits he and Michelle are not together.

11:17 P.M. Rescue workers find Keeler alive.

11:18 P.M. Buchanan calls Logan and suggests that he invokes the 25th Amendment.

11:19 P.M. The couple find the Football and call the police.

11:21 P.M. Tony patches Jack to Jason, who says headlights are coming toward him. Jack tells him to remove the transponder. He does and they run.

11:25 P.M. Marwan arrives and is upset the transponder signal is dead. He does a cell signal sweep.

11:26 P.M. Jack directs the pair to a power station.

11:27 P.M. Marwan tracks them to the station.

11:33 P.M. The couple get shot at by Marwan's men, and a CTU helicopter lands.

11:35 P.M. Jack enters the plant. Jack calls Audrey for the Football code.

11:37 P.M. Jack tells Jason the code and begs them to take the Playbook and the briefcase and separate.

11:45 P.M. Marwan finds Jason and shoots him for the briefcase.

11:46 P.M. Kelly hears Jason's cry. She calls Jack and reveals herself to Marwan.

11:47 P.M. Kelly points to the briefcase. She gives the code. Jack stops henchmen from shooting the couple.

11:55 P.M. Jack and helicopters pursue Marwan. They get the Football but Marwan and pages of the Playbook are missing.

11:58 P.M. Audrey reveals the pages have warhead locations and activation codes.

11:59 P.M. Logan is sworn in and the nuclear threat is still imminent.

Keeler is found alive.

Jack finds the Football.

President Logan gets bad news.

Sean Callery is the Emmy winning composer for *24* and he has been with the series since the pilot. Each season, Callery is faced with creating an overall musical sound for the year, as well as composing individual themes for important central characters to the story. Callery reflects on some of his biggest inspirations of the year, offering, "Marwan was a great villain and they had such tremendous suspenseful sequences with him and running around. There were some great scenes with the Araz family. When Behrooz's girlfriend was poisoned, it was a horrific scene. I remember getting to that show, thinking how am I going to top this because it's so incredible! When I watch an episode, the thing I tend to resist is to make a standard choice musically. When you see a Middle Eastern family living in America, are we going to put Middle Eastern instrumentation in here? In many ways, I thought, it's not about that.

To me, it was almost irrelevant to me that the family was Middle Eastern. It was about a family that was in on an entire plot to attack the country they live in. Yes, it's true, the fact they were of Middle Eastern descent certainly was part of the storyline, but it wasn't the guiding force of the story or the music."

Season four spent a lot of time in the CTU interrogation room with many victims, and Callery says they were some of his favorite scenes to score. "Some of the interrogation scenes in any of the seasons, when you are sitting in a room and you are uncomfortable, musically something might be able to be done almost subconsciously to give that unsettling feeling. I love experimenting with that stuff. Joel [Surnow] gave me great advice [once], saying, "Musically, just tell the story. You don't need to be superfluous." So there are a lot of very minimal moments in 24, but in my opinion, they are as hard to execute as a full on chase scene. My responsibility is to tell the story whether it is a very quiet scene or whether it's a very loud scene."

Research Files

Nuclear Football: When Air Force One goes down in the desert, Jack and Marwan embark on a race to recover the Nuclear Football (a.k.a. the President's Emergency Satchel or The Button). The highly classified black briefcase is a mobile node that allows the President of the United States to order a nuclear attack if away from a fixed command center. While the public is not privy to the exact contents of the case, it is assumed to contain a secure SAT-COM radio and nuclear launch codes. The 'football' nickname is said to be derived from the attack plan coded as Drop Kick. The case is not actually carried by the President, but by one of the rotating Presidential Military Aides, who is an armed commissioned officer in the US Military. The aide is required to maintain a ready distance from the President at all times.

Additional Intel

Jeff Charbonneau is the 24 music editor and it's his job to 'spot' the show. 'Spotting' is when the editor reviews the episode and decides where the composed music is going to be placed within the show.

12:00 am - 1:00 am

Director: Jon Cassar

Writers: Joel Surnow & Michael Loceff

Guest Cast: Jude Ciccolella (Mike Novick), James Morrison (Bill Buchanan), Reiko Aylesworth (Michelle Dessler), Carlos Bernard (Tony Almeida), Arnold Vosloo (Habib Marwan)

"My family and I feel no differently than each and every one of you. We are shocked, saddened...and maybe a little afraid." President Charles Logan

Timeframe

Key Events

12:04 A.M. Marwan cross-references a warhead being shipped to Iowa. They plan to intercept.

12:05 A.M. Chloe alerts that Yosik Khatami just used his credit card and he is linked to Marwan. Curtis heads out.

12:07 A.M. Yosik calls Marwan about his credit card mistake, and he is directed to a marina to escape.

12:08 A.M. Logan retreats to the bunker. He is upset Marwan is at large.

12:12 A.M. Chloe finds Yosik's car.

12:16 A.M. Tony apologizes to Michelle about Buchanan.

12:18 A.M. Curtis and his team arrive at the marina. They ID Yosik and another man, Joe Prado.

12:19 A.M. Prado takes Yosik out on a boat.

12:22 A.M. Agents raid the boat. Yosik calls Marwan, who orders Prado to kill Yosik. Prado tells agents Yosik was trying to steal his boat.

12:24 A.M. Audrey reports a warhead convoy is missing.

12:30 A.M. The ambushed convoy is destroyed and men take the crated warhead on a flatbed.

12:32 A.M. Prado enters CTU. Tony tells Curtis Prado is an ex-Marine.

12:33 A.M. Chloe gets word on the ambush. The torture specialist is brought in for Prado.

12:34 A.M. The interrogation is halted.

12:35 A.M. A lawyer from Amnesty Global arrives with an order to protect Prado.

12:42 A.M. Jack enters CTU and is debriefed. He is furious.

12:43 A.M. Jack confronts the lawyer who will not reveal his source call. They determine the source could be Marwan.

12:46 A.M. Logan is briefed. Novick advises taking action.

12:49 A.M. Jack offers to resign to take on Prado as a citizen.

12:55 A.M. CTU releases Prado. A Marshall escorts him out. Jack tasers the guard and handcuffs Prado.

12:59 A.M. Jack breaks each finger until Prado confesses Marwan's location.

Logan enters the bunker.

Powell is escorted into CTU.

Jack starts breaking fingers.

If there is a recurring theme in season four, it's definitely torture. Whether it's the torture specialist working steadily in the CTU interrogation room all day or just Jack breaking a suspect's fingers for information, there were plenty of examples of extreme prejudice. While it's become an important component of the show, many critics said that writers this season used the device too much. Executive producer Howard Gordon says the writers never use torture without considering and portraying the consequences on screen. "Whether it's issues involving Muslims, involving terrorists, involving torture, we're very aware of it and we never want to trivialize it. Jack's torture as a narrative technique is something we don't want to trivialize either. I think that's really very essential to Jack Bauer's character. Sometimes awful things need to be done to get something done, but Jack Bauer pays a terrible

price on his soul. Sort of our two tropes are torture and immunity. What do you do when you have somebody and you need to stop something from happening? Those are the things we use as narrative devices, so I don't think we ever pretend to advertise the efficacy of torture. I think sometimes the price of that torture is that the wrong information comes out and that there is a human price to be paid for this thing that, obviously, as far as the show is concerned, is necessary because he does get results."

Research Files

Amnesty Global: The lawyer sent to stop Prado's interrogation is from a human rights protection organization. While Amnesty Global doesn't actually exist, it is modeled on Amnesty International (AI), the most widely respected human rights organization in the world. The non-governmental organization says their mandate is "to free all prisoners of conscience; to ensure fair and prompt trials for political prisoners; to abolish the death penalty, torture, and other treatment of prisoners held by international law to be cruel or inhumane; to end political killings and forced disappearances; and to oppose all human rights abuses, whether committed by governments or by other groups." In addition, it has recently expanded its campaigns to include "economic, social and cultural rights". AI retains lawyers to help protect people from human rights violations perpetrated around the globe. Its efforts to protect the unprotected of the world earned it the Nobel Peace Prize in 1977.

Additional Intel

Actress Kim Raver was born and raised in New York City, where she still lives today. As a child she appeared on *Sesame Street* and her breakout adult role was as Kim Zambrano on *Third Watch*, the series she left to work on *24*.

James Heller

Experience:

Department of Defense – Secretary
Member of the President's Cabinet
Anderson Aerospace Corporation – President & CEO
Ballard Technology – CFO
US Ballistic Missile Threat Committee – Counsellor to the President
US Commission to Assess National Security Policy – Chairman
The President's Economic Stabilization Program – Director
United States Congress – Representative
House Armed Services Committee – Chairman
House Appropriations Committee – Member
Applied Aviation Company – President

Education:

Yale University – Bachelor of Arts, Political Science

Military:

US Army – Air Defense Artillery Officer
Pilot and Instructor
Captain, Retired Reserve

Honors:

Presidential Medal of Freedom
Aerospace Executive of the Year
Board of Trustee, National Park Foundation
Board of Trustee, Freedom Foundation
NROTC Scholarship

Personal:

Daughter – Audrey Raines
Son – Richard Heller

Chloe O'Brian

Experience:

CTU – Intelligence Agent, Los Angeles Domestic Unit

CTU – Internet Protocol Manager, Los Angeles Domestic Unit

Expertise:

Built IPSec architecture.

Attacks scripts, computer vulnerabilities, intrusion detection, penetration testing, operational security, viruses.

Proficiency in Cerberus and PlutoPlus.

Education:

University of California (Davis) – Bachelor of Science, Computer Science

Personal:

Divorced

1:00 am - 2:00 am

Director: Bryan Spicer
Writers: Howard Gordon & Evan Katz

Guest Cast: Arnold Vosloo (Habib Marwan), John Allen Nelson (Wa
Cummings), Cameron Bancroft (Lee Castle), Dennis Haysbert
(David Palmer)

> "With all due respect, restraint is a luxury we can't afford right now." Bill Buchanan

Timeframe / Key Events

1:00 A.M. Prado is treated. Audrey is upset Jack is responsible.

1:04 A.M. Audrey confronts Jack. Curtis supports Jack.

1:05 A.M. Logan is frozen with indecision.

1:06 A.M. Buchanan calls Novick to say Jack got the confession anyway.

1:08 A.M. Marwan calls Robert Morrison, who has the warhead. An engineer, Sabir, says the nuke will be operational in an hour.

1:09 A.M. Sabir's girlfriend calls asking if he is involved in the terrorism.

1:11 A.M. Logan hears of Jack's decision and calls for his arrest.

1:18 A.M. Jack and Curtis arrive at a nightclub with SWAT.

1:19 A.M. Sabir's girlfriend calls CTU about her boyfriend.

1:21 A.M. Buchanan calls Jack about the arrest. They can't find Marwan in the club.

1:25 A.M. Marwan's men spot the agents and the cover is blown. Jack sees Marwan and gives chase.

1:29 A.M. The terrorists go into an underground tunnel. A bomb explodes and blocks the tunnel. The Secret Service arrests Jack.

1:35 A.M. Buchanan briefs the President that Marwan is gone because of Jack's arrest. Logan is destroyed and admits he needs help.

1:38 A.M. Novick calls Palmer.

1:45 A.M. Jack is released and goes back to CTU.

1:48 A.M. Marwan escapes from the tunnel.

1:49 A.M. Chloe determines from the girlfriend that Sabir is likely in Iowa. Buchanan orders Chloe to the girl's house to get more locked data.

1:55 A.M. Chloe arrives but her work is interrupted by gunmen.

1:57 A.M. Chloe calls Edgar for help but has to hang up.

1:58 A.M. Chloe and the girl escape into the CTU car. The gunmen fire on them.

1:59 A.M. Chloe unlocks the gun and fires the automatic rifle, killing the gunmen.

Marwan escapes... again.

Palmer is back in the mix.

Chloe blows away the bad guys.

After more than a season and a half of being relegated to the dark workstations of CTU, Chloe O'Brian gets sent out into the field to get data from an informant. Content inside the safety of the CTU set, actress Mary Lynn Rajskub says initially she wasn't so sure about Chloe's field trip. "It was weird. I knew I was going to have to do it a week before we shot it. It's always different than what you expect because you don't know how it is going to be blocked out, especially if you are me. I'm kind of lazy sometimes, so when I read it, I went, 'Oh yeah that's what's going to happen,' and I put the script down."

The episode involved an intricate battle between assassins surrounding the informant's house and culminating in Chloe's badass assault rifle attack on the enemies. Remembering the shoot, Rajskub says, "I got there that night and I have to put together the pieces, because I had to run through that whole

house and the other guy gets shot and we are being chased and running across the street. They added in a scene where the neighbor comes out, which was spontaneous, and then the positioning of the car and the fact that I would have to take the gun out of there. It happens and comes together as you rehearse it, which you do forty minutes before you shoot it really." The actress admits her frontal attack with the gun was the first time she ever had to fire one. "With this show, we move pretty fast so there's not a lot of preparation. It was a couple of hours before I did the gun stuff, and it was, 'Here's a gun. Go stand in the parking lot and try to shoot it.' But it works for the character, because I don't shoot guns. But now I think it would be cool to go through some fight and gun training. It felt pretty good! I was very powerful and kind of scary. It was fun!"

Research Files

Automatic Rifle: When Chloe hits the field for the first time, she does it in a big way, taking out the bad guys with an automatic weapon. She fires an automatic rifle, a self-loading rifle capable of firing either semi- or fully automatically. When the trigger is depressed on a fully automatic rifle, a magazine is fired systematically until the ammunition is spent. A semi-automatic can only fire one bullet each time the trigger is pulled. A semi can be easily converted to a fully automatic rifle. Due to the extreme danger of an automatic rifle, with its barrage of bullets, fully automatic weapons tend to be restricted to military and police organizations. In the US, the Firearm Owners Protection Act of 1986 banned the public from owning machine guns

Additional Intel

24 almost lost actress Mary Lynn Rajskub from the show back in season three, because the producers didn't sign her to a commitment deal. She was free to audition for other shows and she landed a part on *Kelsey Grammer Presents: The Sketch Show*. She remained a guest star on *24* for the rest of the season and was made a season regular for season four.

2:00 a.m - 3:00 a.m

Director: Bryan Spicer
Writer: Peter M. Lenkov

Guest Cast: James Frain (Paul Raines), Gregory Itzin (President Charles Logan), Glenn Morshower (Agent Aaron Pierce), Thomas Vincent Kelly (Dr Benson), Dennis Haysbert (David Palmer)

"When I shot that guy, I thought I'd go all fetal position, but the truth is, I didn't feel anything. At all. I hope I'm not some kind of a psychopath." Chloe O'Brian

Timeframe	Key Events

2:00 A.M. Palmer enters the White House bunker. Logan asks him to be his proxy.

2:06 A.M. Chloe is back forwarding weapons emails to Edgar for sourcing.

2:07 A.M. Edgar connects the emails to a Chinese nuclear researcher named Lee Jong.

2:08 A.M. Audrey tells Paul he needs to go to a spinal hospital.

2:10 A.M. Buchanan tells Jack that Jong is at the Chinese Consulate. Palmer wants to talk to Jack.

2:11 A.M. Palmer says he will try to reason with the Chinese, but if they don't – Jack needs to do whatever it takes to get Jong.

2:12 A.M. Edgar, Michelle and Buchanan determine the detonation will be at dawn.

2:17 A.M. Palmer asks the Chinese Consul in Los Angeles to hand over Jong.

2:24 A.M. Palmer calls Jack and says desperate measures must be taken. Jack takes the unofficial assignment to get Jong.

2:25 A.M. Jack confides in Tony about the mission.

2:31 A.M. Wearing a mask, Jack enters the Consulate and Tony guides him through the guard stations.

2:33 A.M. Jack immobilizes Jong and carries him out. Guards start firing. Curtis and his masked agents help Jack out.

2:35 A.M. Jong is hit and critical.

2:36 A.M. Paul's heart starts filling with blood and surgery is necessary again.

2:43 A.M. Jack, through a translator, asks Jong how to find Marwan. Jong demands a Presidential pardon first.

2:46 A.M. Palmer promises to get the pardon and then lies to the Chinese Deputy Consul about the raid.

2:47 A.M. Palmer is very concerned about future Chinese relations if the link is revealed.

2:55 A.M. Jack wheels Jong into where Paul is in the middle of surgery. Jack demands the doctor work on Jong immediately.

2:57 A.M. Paul crashes and dies.

2:59 A.M. Audrey says Jack killed Paul.

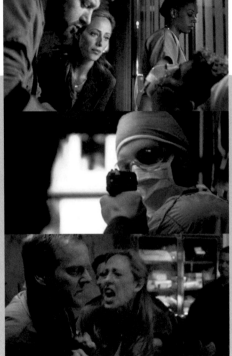

Paul is rushed back into surgery.

Jack demands the surgeon's help.

Audrey blames Jack for Paul's death.

Actress Kim Raver says this episode was the highlight of the season for her for a few reasons. "When Kiefer and I have scenes there is just such a great... I don't know. It's really special when you can do your homework as an actor and you walk in the door and you have someone as giving as Kiefer. You know you've got your homework to back you up, but then it becomes a whole other rich scene, especially working with directors like Jon Cassar. The three of us just love it. We just dive into the scenes, especially in episode twenty, where Jack has to make the choice to save a lot of American lives or the life of my ex-husband. Just shooting that was really amazing. It's all terrific stuff that they write, but there are definitely scenes that stick in your mind.

"There is another moment in episode twenty, where Jack does make that decision and kills [Audrey's] ex-husband," she

continues. "It was huge. We really sat down. Kiefer had some very strong opinions and I had some very strong opinions and so did Jon. It was really great because we all voiced what our instincts where on it and how to get to where we need to get to. I said, 'My instincts are that I am just going to go after you!' Kiefer was like, 'Yeah!' But I said, 'I can't slap you!' He was like, 'You are going to have to!' I was really slapping him in that. On a personal level it was really hard, but it was really physical and emotional. We did it over and over. It's funny because there was a point where we all realized we needed one more take and Kiefer was like, 'F***! Remember guys, you are slapping me!' He's incredible that way because he knew it would work really well and we went for it. I love that day because it was so collaborative and everyone had such strong opinions and we had the time to really rehearse it."

Research Files

Chinese Consulate: In the United States, foreign representatives that oversee the interests of their country and citizens are known officially as 'diplomatic missions' and are located in Washington DC. A permanent mission is called an embassy and the person in charge of that representation is known as an ambassador. Across the rest of the nation in larger cities, there are consulates that work in tangent with their embassies to handle the business or personal needs of their citizens within the United States. A consul is a representative of a sovereign state working at their consulate. The primary function of a consulate lies in promoting their domestic trade, helping their business interests in selling goods in the host country or city, as well as importing goods. A consulate's other unofficial function is to acquire intelligence about the host city for their embassy.

Additional Intel

Kiefer Sutherland admitted that when he was filming the scene where he is climbing the Chinese Consulate wall, his gun fell out of his pocket and discharged, shooting a blank into his butt.

3:00 a.m - 4:00 a.m.

Director: Kevin Hooks

Writers: Joel Surnow & Michael Loceff

Guest Cast: Tzi Ma (Cheng Zhi), Keith Szarabajka (Robert Morrison), Robert Cicchini (Howard Bern), Gwendoline Yeo (Melissa Raab), Dennis Haysbert (David Palmer)

"Chloe, we're in an active code. We don't have time for your personality disorder, you understand me?" Bill Buchanan

Timeframe | Key Events

3:00 A.M. Jack apologizes to Audrey. She tells him to go.

3:06 A.M. Chloe determines someone is trying to jam CTU satellites.

3:07 A.M. Marwan wants to move the deadline up an hour.

3:08 A.M. Palmer and Novick decide to blame the raid on Asian extremists.

3:09 A.M. The Chinese head of security IDs one of the SWAT agents.

3:10 A.M. Jack talks to the team about alibis.

3:11 A.M. Marwan attaches the nuke to a missile.

3:17 A.M. Audrey gives Jack DoD clearance for data transfer.

3:19 A.M. The Chinese Deputy Consul calls Michelle about the raid and blames CTU.

3:23 A.M. Logan is furious with Palmer for allowing the raid. Palmer is unapologetic.

3:28 A.M. Michelle says the Chinese Head of Security, Cheng, is heading to CTU.

3:30 A.M. Tony and Michelle admit they still love each other. Cheng arrives.

3:31 A.M. Jack dresses in a suit and fields Cheng's questions.

3:34 A.M. Jack has Chloe prep a getaway helicopter for the exposed CTU agent.

3:35 A.M. Jong gives three addresses of where Marwan might be in LA.

3:43 A.M. Jack explains the whole story to Audrey.

3:45 A.M. Audrey lies to Cheng for Jack.

3:48 A.M. Logan accuses Novick and Palmer of plotting against him, but he quickly folds and agrees Cheng should be taken out of CTU.

3:55 A.M. On his way out, Cheng hears Edgar talk about the raid and he determines Jack was behind the attack.

3:57 A.M. Jack enters Marwan's building and shoots the terrorist in the arm. Marwan tells him the missile is already set. It fires – destination unknown.

Cheng grills CTU on the raid.

Edgar spills to Cheng.

Marwan is under Jack's gun.

One of the slimier characters to come out of the season is President Charles Logan. Thrown into the role of President after the attack on Air Force One and the grave injuries to President Keeler, Logan quickly proved to be a man poorly suited to the role of Commander in Chief of the United States. Originally, the character grew out of a need to get David Palmer back into play. Executive producer and co-creator Robert Cochran explains, "We wanted to bring Palmer back because we missed him and we knew the fans missed him and we love [Dennis] Haysbert. We thought, 'What if the new President is in over his head? He makes some mistakes and then has the sense to call in Palmer.' So really the creation of President Logan was a way of bringing Palmer back, and then we began to love the character of Charles Logan because Gregory Itzin did such a great job with the character. It was a

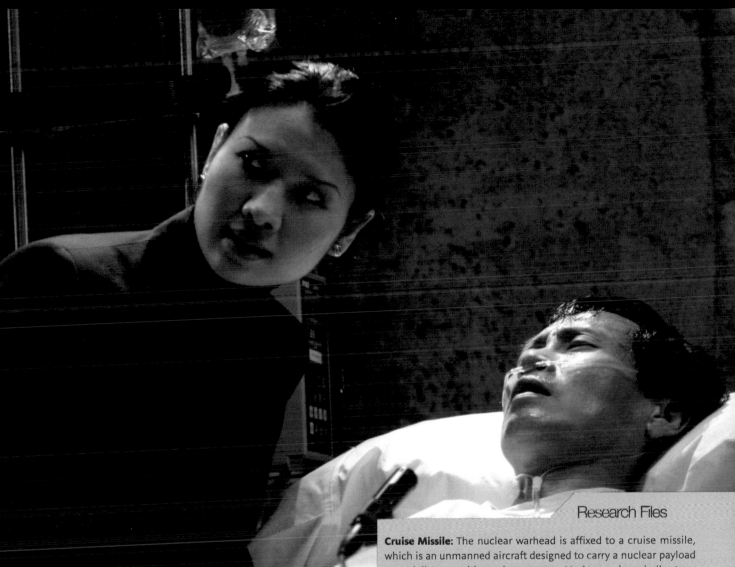

device to bring Palmer back but we said, 'Let's stay with it,' and that's the genesis of Charles Logan."

Gregory Itzin's pitch-perfect portrayal of a weak man with way too much power often drew comparisons to real life former President Richard Nixon. The actor says that he never patterned the character on Nixon, offering, "I'm not modeling myself after anybody. When I was first approached about doing this, they said, 'We're not sure where he's going. He has a hard time making a decision.' And so they wrote it, and I gave them choices from semi-staunch leader of men to abject coward, and they always kept writing towards the abject coward. Those words kept coming up, and those things kept coming up. So I suppose intellectually you start thinking about any parallels with leaders in the past. But mostly it's the lines that bring this thing to fruition, not me trying to be like anybody else."

Research Files

Cruise Missile: The nuclear warhead is affixed to a cruise missile, which is an unmanned aircraft designed to carry a nuclear payload a good distance with precise accuracy. Modern cruise missiles travel at supersonic speeds at low altitude to avoid radar detection. They can be launched from ships, aircraft or mobile launchers on the ground. The first cruise missile was created in 1917 for World War One, but the war was over before it was deployed. During World War Two, Nazi Germany used a cruise missile known as the V-1 starting in 1944. In the late fifties, the US funded a project known as Project Pluto to create a nuclear cruise missile. In modern times, cruise missiles are among the most expensive of single-use weapons, costing about a million dollars per deployment.

Additional Intel

Originally, *24* producers planned to shoot the White House scenes on the set used for the television series *The West Wing*. The budget didn't work out so production designer Joseph Hodges built a partial set of a portion of the White House.

4:00 am - 5:00 am

Director: Kevin Hooks

Writers: Matt Michnovetz & Duppy Demetrius

Guest Cast: Reiko Aylesworth (Michelle Dessler), Gregory Itzin (President Charles Logan), Robert Cicchini (Howard Burn), Gwendoline Yeo (Melissa Raab)

"The last thing I ever wanted to do was push you away from me. God, Audrey, I love you, but this is how the job has to be done." Jack Bauer

Timeframe / Key Events

4:00 A.M. The missile can't be traced.

4:01 A.M. Jack calls Palmer and is concerned he won't be able to break Marwan.

4:06 A.M. Edgar finds a call from Richard Heller on Marwan's cell phone.

4:07 A.M. Chloe briefs Buchanan on the link and they call Heller.

4:08 A.M. Audrey refuses to believe her brother is connected.

4:09 A.M. A grenade is launched at the CTU agents so the terrorists are able to take Marwan.

4:16 A.M. Logan addresses the Cabinet but they quickly realize Palmer is silently in charge.

4:20 A.M. Richard is brought back into CTU. Audrey begs to talk to him first.

4:30 A.M. Heller arrives and sees Audrey is failing with Richard. He gets his son to admit he hooked up with a couple last week and the woman may have used his phone.

4:33 A.M. Heller is livid Richard jeopardized national security.

4:39 A.M. Chloe tracks down the couple. Edgar determines Richard's phone was compromised so the terrorists could track him and his family.

4:40 A.M. Logan returns to his Cabinet and proceeds to put Palmer in his place in front of everyone. The performance sells the Cabinet on Logan's authority.

4:42 A.M. As Tony prepares to leave to get Jack, Michelle says she will quit to be with Tony.

4:44 A.M. Jack calls Audrey expressing his love and sorrow.

4:46 A.M. Mandy the assassin and Gary finish having sex and hear a helicopter.

4:48 A.M. Mandy shoots Gary and prepares to escape.

4:55 A.M. Jack enters the apartment and finds Gary dead.

4:57 A.M. Mandy kills an agent and takes Tony hostage. Richard IDs the woman.

4:58 A.M. Jack fears the operation is compromised as Michelle listens in fear.

Tony and Michelle reunite.

Mandy the assassin is back!

Mandy takes Tony hostage.

Casting director Debi Manwiller says casting the role of Habib Marwan was one of their department's biggest headaches in season four because the producers decided to expand the character at the last minute. "Originally, Marwan had one scene on the phone. He was in a remote location, like Bangkok or something. We asked the producers, 'Will this character come back?' 'No.' 'Will he ever have scenes with Jack?' 'No.' He ended up in seventeen episodes!" Casting associate Peggy Kennedy adds, "What they were saying was Marwan was going to be seen in phone conversations in two episodes, maybe one more, and then he was supposed to be killed in episode ten." "He was not a big mastermind," Manwiller continues. "He was just like any other character, like filler! We actually hired another actor based on what was on the page. What happened is that once we cast the actor, we hadn't shot it yet, and about a week or

so later [the producers] came down and said, 'For that Marwan character, we are going to need blah, blah, blah' and we told them we had already hired the actor and we would have to recast because the actor was not physically right for the role. Through no fault of his own we replaced him with Arnold Vosloo, who is *huge!*" she laughs. After *The Mummy* films, Vosloo had said publicly that he wasn't interested in playing villain roles anymore, but Kennedy says *24* became the exception for him. "Yes, usually, in the past, he did not want to play a bad guy, but it was such an interesting character and you actually did kind of like him. Matter of fact, he was actually supposed to test for a pilot [during the season] and he just said to his agent, 'Don't push that. I'm really happy where I am on *24*.'"

Research Files

Presidential Line of Succession: When President Keeler is taken alive but injured from the Air Force One wreckage, Vice President Charles Logan is sworn into office soon after to fulfill the duties of the Executive Office. The Presidential Succession Act of 1947 determined the line of succession in the event neither a President nor Vice President is able to 'discharge the powers and duties of the office'. The next person in line for the job is the Speaker of the House of Representatives, followed by President *pro tempore* of the Senate, and then the Secretary of State. In total, the line of succession includes fourteen Cabinet members. The only Cabinet member not listed in the line is the Secretary of Homeland Security. In 1963, after the assassination of Kennedy, the Twenty-fifth Amendment to the Constitution was submitted and ratified by the states, which permitted the President to nominate a Vice President, should the Vice Presidency become vacant.

Additional Intel

Actor Arnold Vosloo was born in South Africa, where he became an acclaimed theater and film actor. In the late nineties, he moved to the United States where his first film of note was Ridley Scott's *1492: Conquest of Paradise*. He is best known for playing High Priest Imhotep in *The Mummy* and *The Mummy Returns*.

5:00 am - 6:00 am

Director: Jon Cassar
Writer: Sam Montgomery

Guest Cast: Reiko Aylesworth (Michelle Dessler), Carlos Bernard (Tony Almeida), Dennis Haysbert (David Palmer), Mia Kirshner (Mandy)

> "You put Michelle Dessler's life ahead of national security. You let a suspect escape, and you committed treason. Is she gonna do the same for you?" Mandy

Timeframe

Key Events

5:03 A.M. Mandy holds Tony in an empty apartment.

5:04 A.M. Marwan calls Mandy about their meeting. She wonders if Michelle will commit treason for Tony.

5:05 A.M. Audrey is asked to compile disaster scenarios for 20 cities.

5:07 A.M. Mandy contacts Michelle demanding her help in escaping or she kills Tony.

5:14 A.M. Michelle tells Buchanan about the call.

5:15 A.M. Buchanan calls Jack and they work out a plan.

5:19 A.M. Mandy tasers Tony and goes outside. She shoots a neighbor and goes inside.

5:27 A.M. The compromised CTU agent calls to confirm he is in San Diego with a new alibi. Cheng is waiting for him. The Chinese security head demands the agent's confession.

5:31 A.M. Mandy calls Michelle, who says the agents are cleared out.

5:33 A.M. Jack watches a couple approach a car. Mandy sees the agents. The car explodes.

5:38 A.M. Buchanan calls the President. The missile can't be traced. Palmer has CTU shift to disaster management.

5:41 A.M. Buchanan sends Michelle home.

5:44 A.M. Jack figures out Mandy made the call from inside where she could see the car. He has Curtis alert the teams.

5:45 A.M. Mandy sees CTU has caught on. As they leave, Tony steps on glass to leave a trail of blood.

5:51 A.M. Agents find the blood and alert Jack.

5:52 A.M. Tony attacks Mandy, but she is able to get the upper hand again.

5:53 A.M. Jack arrives and there is a standoff. Curtis arrives and grabs Mandy. Jack calls CTU.

5:54 A.M. Tony calls Michelle.

5:56 A.M. Jack puts Mandy in a chokehold and offers a pardon if she reveals Marwan now.

5:57 A.M. Cheng threatens to send the agent to Siberia. He relents and implicates Jack Bauer.

Tony and Mandy blown up?

Jack chokes Mandy for info.

Jack Bauer is implicated.

The personal stakes for Michelle Dessler and Tony Almeida come to a head with Mandy the assassin holding him hostage. Actress Reiko Aylesworth says the pressure cooker storyline showed another side to Michelle. "I like the fact in season four that I wasn't as in control towards the end when I think I may be losing my husband. I start screaming at people who really could help me if I wasn't turning against them. I lose it a little and that's always fun to play and it's true. It's so satisfying to have these people doing their best to do their jobs. They've exhausted everything and they can't not say something or kiss them or scream. That's where the passion comes from. The context of our show is great. It's not like we are hanging out saying, 'Hey you look cute today.' It's like, 'F***! We are going to die! I love you!' It's this larger than life situation."

Both Tony and Michelle survive the ordeal, but Aylesworth

never expected that outcome. "I was certain they were sacrificing one of us and I thought it was going to be me! They *were* going to kill me and they actually ran it by me," she reveals. "I've always been fine with getting killed. It's not a show you can get too attached to. It's just the manner in which I get killed. I actually went up to them in the beginning and asked, 'So, how ya gonna do it?' I just had a problem with, and I think a lot of people had a problem with, the way they wanted to kill me off. They were tossing around the idea of having me commit suicide. I went in and said, 'Oh... okay. Why? That is so not Michelle.' I just thought, they wrote this great character, why undercut her? She's not crazy and she's not fourteen. They wanted to do this *Romeo & Juliet* thing, and yes, we have a great love, but it's not the character at all. I said, 'I don't mind you killing me. I just don't want to go out weak.' I think in the end, I think they realized, 'Wait, a minute... no one is expecting a happy ending!'"

Research Files

Siberia: The Chinese consul threatens to secretly banish the CTU agent to Siberia, which has long been held as a terrifying fate for anyone. Located in Russia, Siberia is a large portion of the country consisting of almost all of Northeast Asia. A vast wasteland filled with natural resources, Siberia was unexplored for a long period of its history until the construction of the Trans-Siberian Railway, which opened in 1903. The Soviet Union opened notorious prison camps in the region called gulags, which became so full that eventually the region came to be used as a metaphor for exile and punishment. The geography of Siberia is so vast that it has a population density of only three people per square kilometer. Seventy percent of the population lives in cities, in the south along the railway route. Oymyakon has the lowest recorded temperature of −71°C, making it the coldest town on Earth.

Additional Intel

24 won three Emmy's for season four: Outstanding Single-Camera Sound Mixing for a Series, Outstanding Sound Editing for a Series, and Outstanding Stunt Coordination.

6:00 am - 7:00 am

Director: Jon Cassar

Writers: Robert Cochran & Howard Gordon

Guest Cast: Mia Kirshner (Mandy), John Allen Nelson (Walt Cummings), Dennis Haysbert (David Palmer), Arnold Vosloo (Habib Marwan)

> "This is probably the last time we'll ever speak. Jack, you do understand, when you hang up, for all intents and purposes, Jack Bauer's dead." David Palmer

Timeframe

6:01 A.M. Palmer urges Logan to sign the pardon.

6:03 A.M. Mandy says Marwan is on the Global Center roof.

6:05 A.M. Marwan doesn't wait for Mandy. Edgar sends Jack the chopper location.

6:06 A.M. Jack and CTU choppers block Marwan's escape.

6:07 A.M. Marwan flees. He kills an agent and wounds Curtis.

6:09 A.M. Marwan tries to jump off the building, but Jack grabs him. Marwan takes out a knife and slices Jack's hand until he slips to his death.

6:17 A.M. The acting Chinese Consul calls and reveals they have the agent's confession on video. They want Jack.

6:19 A.M. Agents upload the damaged data device to CTU.

6:20 A.M. Edgar and Chloe uncover a flight path.

6:22 A.M. An F-18 spots the missile and shoots it down successfully.

6:27 A.M. Michelle and Tony emotionally reunite.

6:29 A.M. Audrey breaks up with Jack. He is devastated.

6:31 A.M. Palmer calls Jack and explains the Chinese situation. Secret Service is on its way to arrest Jack.

6:33 A.M. Walt Cummings insinuates Agent Spaulding should kill Jack. Novick overhears.

6:40 A.M. Palmer fails to reason with Logan.

6:42 A.M. Palmer calls Jack with a warning to get out of CTU.

6:45 A.M. Tony tells Buchanan that Jack is in Section C.

6:50 A.M. Spaulding is upset and Buchanan orders him to take Tony to go find Jack.

6:51 A.M. Jack fires at the pair. Tony finds Jack in a pool of blood and Spaulding confirms Jack is dead. Buchanan takes Spaulding out.

6:53 A.M. Tony revives Jack. They plan to switch bodies.

6:55 A.M. Audrey talks to Buchanan and finds out Jack is dead.

6:57 A.M. Tony and Michelle drop Jack off at a railroad track with new ID, a bag and a secure phone.

6:58 A.M. Jack calls Palmer and they say goodbye.

6:59 A.M. Jack dons sunglasses and disappears.

Key Events

Jack hangs onto Marwan.

Audrey says goodbye to Jack.

Jack Bauer disappears...

The image of Jack Bauer walking away from his life to start anew in the anonymity of his 'death' is one of the most poignant moments ever on the series. As a new day dawns over Los Angeles, the season comes to a close, and the future for Jack is absolutely uncertain leading into season five. Actor Kiefer Sutherland says he loved the ending and where it left Bauer emotionally. "Dramatically [his death] was an amazing device. What was really interesting was for David Palmer's character it was sad because he was losing a friend, for all the other people it was also sad that they were losing a friend, but for Jack Bauer, outside of the loss of his daughter – and even in that circumstance he thought it was safer for her – it was almost like freedom. He was the one character that got to walk away from that [situation], almost as a relief."

Often quoted as saying *24* could continue to have a life

Research Files

Slowing the Heart: In order to get Jack out of being arrested by the Chinese for his part in the consulate raid, the CTU team slows Jack's heart so that his pulse cannot be felt and he can fake death. Beta-blockers block the action in the nerves of the involuntary nervous system and reduce the heart rate. Blocking these receptors prevents the action of two chemicals called noradrenaline and adrenaline that occur naturally in the body. For the second time in the series, Jack is revived by Epinephrine, a hormone and a neurotransmitter that increases heart rate, dilates the pupils, and constricts arterioles in the skin and gut while dilating arterioles in leg muscles. It also elevates the blood sugar level and is used to revive cardiac arrest patients.

Additional Intel

Season four racked up the highest death count of all seasons to date. By hour twenty-four, 225 people were dead and Jack Bauer killed 39 of them.

without his character on the show anymore, Sutherland admits that the finale of season four was one of the first times he really considered that possibility. "After doing the show for as long as we have, certainly it was the beginning of that point," the actor reveals. "After fours years, it's a long time for a show to be on the air. So absolutely, I thought about it. I remember walking onto the stage towards the end of season four thinking, 'Wow, when this is over someday, it's going to be a sad day for me because I have enjoyed it so much.' Then your fifteen minutes of alone time is over and you have to go back to work," he laughs. "So, yes, they are short-lived thoughts, and when it does end for me it will be a sad day."

INTO SEASON FIVE

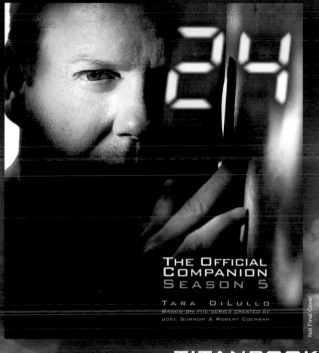
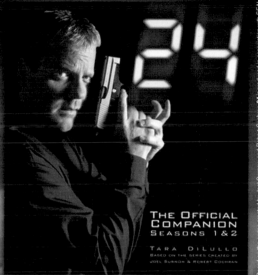

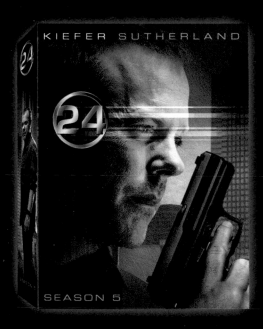

DON'T TAKE YOUR EYES OFF HIM.
NOT EVEN FOR A SECOND.

KIEFER SUTHERLAND

24

SEASON 5

24 SEASON 5
AVAILABLE NOW

*Loaded with hours of
Special Features including
DVD exclusive 11-minute short
bridging Seasons 5 and 6,
23 Extended/Deleted Scenes
and DVD-ROM Link to
exclusive online content.*